SACRED SONGS OF INDIA

VOLUME EIGHT

BOOKS BY V.K. SUBRAMANIAN

The Upanishads and the Bible

Introspection for India—A Paradigm for Progress

Sacred Songs of India (Vols. I, II, III, IV, V, VI, VII, VIII, IX & X)

The Holistic Way to Health, Happiness and Harmony

Wondrous Whispers of Wisdom from Ancient India (Vols. I, II & III)

Predictive Planets and Presaging Palms

Maxims of Chanakya

Saundaryalahari

Sivanandalahari

Sri Rudraprasna

The Indian Financial System

The Great Ones (Vols. I, II & III)

Lali and Other Short Stories

Love Twigs

A Bond to Sorrow

A Feeling for Feminism

Art of Ancient India: Some Moving Mementoes

SACRED SONGS OF INDIA

VOLUME EIGHT

V.K. SUBRAMANIAN

ABHINAV PUBLICATIONS

abhinav publications

Cataloging in Publication Data--DK
Courtesy: D.K. Agencies (P) Ltd. <docinfo@dkagencies.com>

Sacred songs of India / [translated by] V.K. Subramanian.
v. 8 cm.
Texts in Indian languages (Devanagari and roman); translation and introductory matter in English.
Selections from the lifework of mystic musician-saints of India; on love and devotion towards their favourite deities.
ISBN 8170174325 (v. 8)

1. Sacred songs. 2. Hindu saints--Songs and music. 3. Bhajans. 4. Songs--India. 5. Devotional poetry, Indic--Translations into English. I. Subramanian, V. K. (Vadakaymadam Krishnier), 1930-

DDC 782.250 954 21

First Published in India 2006

Publishers
Shakti Malik
Abhinav Publications
E-37, Hauz Khas
New Delhi-110016 (INDIA)
Phones: 26566387, 26562784, 26524658
Fax: 91-11-26857009
e-mail: shakti@nde.vsnl.net.in
website: http://www.abhinavexports.com

ISBN 81-7017-432-5

Printed at
D.K. Fine Art Press P. Ltd.

To
my son, Anand
(officially known as V.S. Krishnan)
whose honesty, integrity and geniality
make me a proud father

CONTENTS

	Acknowledgements	9
	Introduction	11
1.	Songs of Tirumoolar (3rd-5th Century A.D.)	17
2.	Songs of Kalidasa (6th Century A.D.)	41
3.	Songs of Kulasekhara Perumal (6th-7th Century A.D.)	93
4.	Songs of Kamban (9th Century A.D.)	117
5.	Songs of Devara Dasimayya (10th Century A.D.)	141
6.	Songs of Guru Ramdas (1534 A.D.-1581 A.D.)	165
7.	Songs of Rahim (16th Century A.D.)	191
8.	Songs of Appayya Dikshitar (16th-17th Century A.D.)	213
9.	Songs of Bhima Bhoi (1849 A.D.-1894 A.D.)	241
10.	Songs of Sri Narayana Guru (1856 A.D.-1928 A.D.)	273

ACKNOWLEDGEMENTS

In the compilation of this eighth volume of the Sacred Songs of India, I am indebted to the following friends for their invaluable help:

Mrs. B. Jayalakshmi, for selecting the songs of Kulasekhara Perumal, Tirumoolar and Kamban.

Sri S. Sampath Kumar, for help in translation of the songs of Tirumoolar, Kulasekhara Perumal and Kamban.

Dr. Manjula Sriram, Lecturer, Music Academy College of Music, Chennai, for selecting the songs of Devara Dasimayya.

Mrs. Nandini Kapdi, I.A.A.S., for helping me in the translation of the songs of Devara Dasimayya.

Sri Sarad Mahapatra, Minneapolis and *Sitakant Mahapatra,* I.A.S. (Retd.), for selecting and translating the Oriya songs of Bhima Bhoi.

V.K. Subramanian

KEY TO TRANSLITERATION AND PRONUNCIATION

Devanagari letter	Transliterated as	Sounds like	Devanagari letter	Transli-terated as	Sounds like
अ	a	o in son	ड	ḍ	d in den
आ	ā or aa	a in master	ढ	ḍh	dh in childhood
इ	i	i in if	ण	ṇ	n in under
ई	ī or ee	ee in feel	त	t	t in French
उ	u	u in full	थ	th	th in thumb
ऊ	ū	oo in boot	द	d	th in mother
ऋ	ṛ	somewhat between r & ri	ध	dh	th in breathe
ए	e	ay in May	न	n	n in not
ऐ	ai	y in my	प	p	p in pen
ओ	o	o in oh	फ	ph	ph in loophole
औ	au	ow in now	ब	b	b in bag
क	k	k in keen	भ	bh	bh in abhor
ख	kh	ckh in blackhead	म	m	m in mother
ग	g	g in go	य	y	y in yard
घ	gh	gh in loghout	र	r	r in run
ङ	ng	ng in singer	ल	l	l in luck
च	c or ch	ch in chart	व	v	v in avert
छ	ch or cch	ch in chain	श	ś	ch in Reich
ज	j	j in judge	ष	ṣ or sh	sh in show
झ	jh	dgeh in hedgehog	स	s	s in sun
ञ	ñ	n (somewhat) in French	ह	h	h in hot
ट	ṭ	t in ten	ळ	ḷ	ll in pull
ठ	ṭh	th in anthill	ऴ	zh	j in jean (French)

INTRODUCTION

This volume SACRED SONGS OF INDIA VOLUME EIGHT represents the eighth milestone in my voyage of discovery of the devotional lyrics of the mystic saints of India, who lived in different regions of India, in different periods of India's chequered history and sang in different languages.

I have been elevated by my association with the lives and work of these mystics, whose passionate yearning to unite with the infinite Divine has a running thread of unity, which transcended the barriers of class, caste, gender, language, region and time.

The mystic poet sages included in this volume are: *Tirumoolar*, *Kalidasa*, *Kulasekhara Perumal*, *Kamban*, *Devara Dasimayya*, *Guru Ramdas*, *Rahīm*, *Appayya Dikshitar*, *Bhima Bhoi* and *Sri Narayana Guru*.

They lived between the third century A.D. and the twentieth century A.D.

They came from such diverse regions of India as Tamil Nadu, Punjab, Orissa, Madhya Pradesh, Kerala, Karnataka and Uttar Pradesh.

They sang in Sanskrit, Tamil, Punjabi, Hindi, Oriya and Malayalam.

Tirumoolar, who lived probably between the third and fifth century A.D., is the pioneer of the system of devotion known as *Saiva Siddhānta*, which was nurtured by the Saivite saints of Tamil Nadu, known as ***Nāyanmars***. Tirumoolar's *magnum opus* is the classic work *Tirumantiram*, which contains 3000 verses and deals with the Yoga path to liberation.

Tirumoolar is unique among the mystics in stressing the importance of the body as a vehicle for spiritual uplift.

He emphasised the oneness of humankind and the fact that God is love and also that God was immanent within the human body.

Nevertheless, God to Tirumoolar was the Divine Manifestation: Siva, the Auspicious One, whose dance symbolised the moving phantasmagoria of the cosmos.

Kalidasa, the greatest Sanskrit poet, who lived in the sixth century A.D., during the Golden Age of the Guptas and probably during the reign of King Vikramaditya, revelled in sensory enjoyment and treated life as a festival.

His outstanding literary output is attributed to the grace of the Divine Mother, to whom Kalidasa poured out his devotion and gratitude in the immortal prayer: *Syāmala Dandakam* (included in this volume), a devotional song recited throughout the length and breadth of India by all, old and young, who seek literary skills and success in scholastic studies.

Kalidasa worshipped God as Father-Mother, as indicated in his famous benedictory invocation in the work *Raghuvamsa*:

वागर्थाविव संपृक्तौ वागर्थप्रतिपत्तये।
जगतः पितरौ वन्दे पार्वती परमेश्वरौ॥

Vāgarthāviva sampṛktau vāgarthapratipattaye,
Jagataḥ pitarau vandé pārvatī parameśvarau.

"I bow to the parents of the universe, *Pārvatī* and *Parameśvara,* who are as united as words and their meaning, so that I may attain skill in words and their interpretation."

The three benedictory invocations in honour of

Lord Siva, the Auspicious One, preceding the three plays *Mālavikāgnimitram, Vikramorvasiyam* and *Śākuntalam* are unmatched for their poetic majesty and humble devotion. They are a veritable spiritual treat, when sung melodiously. These have been included in this volume.

Also included is Kalidasa's famous *Navaratnamala,* a song in nine verses in honour of the Divine Mother.

Kulasekhara Perumal the Kerala King who lived in the 6th-7th century A.D. is one of the twelve *Alwars,* the Vaishnavite saints of Tamil Nadu.

It is amazing that Kulasekhara Perumal was so proficient with the Tamil language in his devotional songs.

The intensity of devotion in his case made him identify himself with the characters in religious lore.

Thus, in one of his songs, he expresses empathy with the lot of *Devaki,* Krishna's biological mother from whom Krishna was separated and sent to foster parents in Brindavan: *Nanda* and *Yasoda.*

In another song, he expresses anguish at the lot of Rama who had to wander in the forest for fourteen years, at the behest of his step mother.

Such intensity of devotion is unparalleled and makes Kulasekhara Perumal one of the greatest *Alwars* and a mystic who expresses symbolically the anguish of the devotee in being separated from the Beloved, God.

Devara Dasimayya, the Karnataka saint who lived in the tenth century A.D., was the earliest poet to introduce the *Vacana* form of devotional song, which expresses in short verses the intensity of devotion of the mystic sage.

Later savants of the *Veerasaivite* movement like *Basavanna, Allama Prabhu* and *Mahadevi Akka* fully utilised this form in their devotional songs.

Guru Ramdas, the fourth Sikh Guru who lived between 1534 A.D. and 1581 A.D. continued the tradition of earlier Gurus in stressing the importance of chanting the Lord's name as a means to get rid of the ills that afflict mortal life and attain union with God. The unmistakable influence of Vaishnavism continues to be seen in the songs of Guru Ramdas as in the case of other Sikh Gurus.

To Guru Ramdas, as to other Sikh Gurus, God was: *Hari, Rama, Govind, Madhusudan, Murari, Narahari* etc.: names which are music to the ears of Vaishnavite saints like the *Alwars.*

Rahim, the Muslim mystic, who lived in the 16th century A.D.—a contemporary of Emperor Akbar and saint Tulsidas—was madly in love with the cloud-hued form of Krishna, the Lover of the cowherdesses and described His amoral exploits with devotion and poetic skill.

Appayya Dikshitar, who lived in the 16th-17th century A.D., was a renowned scholar and mystic poet of South India.

He was, like many other mystics of India, diffident about the adequacy of his love and devotion for God. To test his devotion, he drank a poisonous drink which made him delirious. What came out of him in the delirious state would indicate correctly what was really in his heart!

The words which came out of Appayya Dikshitar were taken down by his disciples. These turned out to be the fifty verses called *Ātmārpana Stuti* (Hymn of self-surrender), selections from which are included in this volume.

As can be seen, these verses are soaked in devotion and desperately plead with the Lord to save the devotee.

Bhima Bhoi, the blind tribal mystic, who lived between 1849 A.D. and 1894 A.D., is in a class by himself.

While most mystics poured out their devotion to some specific divine manifestation like Krishna, Rama, Siva, Ganesa or Subrahmania, Bhima Bhoi preferred to adore Him as the formless, elusive One, who pervades everything as the unseen Power. His spiritual path is termed *Mahima Dharma.*

Sri Narayana Guru, the poet sage of Kerala, who lived between 1856 A.D. and 1928 A.D. was basically a social reformer who stood for abolition of caste distinctions. His famous exhortation was: "*One caste, One religion, One God!*" Like the Advaitic philosopher Sankaracharya, Narayana Guru believed in the omnipresence and immanence of God.

Yet, like Sankaracharya, he composed beautiful devotional songs to various manifestations of Divinity like Ganesa, Subrahmania, Siva, the Divine Mother, etc. which, as can be seen from the selections in this volume, are so full of spiritual fervour and philosophic truths.

Thus, in this volume, we have a wonderful fare, comprising the life work of mystics who were kings as well as poor tribal folk, poets who were literary giants like Kalidasa and Kamban and others who, regardless of their professed religion, adored God in unconventional ways.

Once again, it is my privilege and good fortune to present the songs of these mystics, who came from such varied backgrounds and from such different periods of time, and yet through whose outpourings runs the common thread of God-intoxication.

I welcome my readers to savour with relish this ambrosial cocktail of spirituality.

V.K. Subramanian

SONGS OF TIRUMOOLAR

Song	*Raga*
1. Teeyinum veyyan	Hamsadhwani
2. Chooduvan nenjidai vaippan	Kamboji
3. Anpum sivamum	Yamuna Kalyani
4. Ullam perunkoil	Suddha Dhanyasi
5. Padamaada koyil	Sahana
6. Vedangalaada	Ritigowla
7. Maanikkakkoottanai	Sankarabharanam
8. Aaadiya kalum	Mohanam
9. Unarvum avane	Sindhu Bhairavi
10. Nirampala evvannam	Madhyamavati

TIRUMOOLAR

TIRUMOOLAR (3rd Century-5th Century A.D.)

Tirumoolar is deemed the Doyen of mystics and seers of Tamil Nadu.

The spiritual path shown by Tirumoolar became, nurtured by the *Nayanmars*, the system of devotion famous as *Saiva Siddhanta*, which was propagated by a number of mystics, the latest being Ramalinga Swamigal who lived in the 19th century A.D.

Tirumoolar's *magnum opus* is *Tirumantiram*, a work comprising 3000 verses.

Tirumoolar's most profound dictum was: *Anbe Sivam*, "God is Love." Adoration of God is hence cardinal to Tirumoolar.

The other famous dictum of Tirumoolar is: *Yan petra Inbam peruka Ivvaiyakam* viz. "May this world experience the bliss I have experienced."

The third dictum of Tirumoolar is: *Onre kulamum Oruvane Daivamum*: "Mankind is one family. There is only one God."

Tirumoolar also propagated the view that the body, being the temple of God, was to be treasured as a divine gift.

Tirumoolar realised the presence of God within and adored Him as the immanent presence.

Tirumoolar's emphasis on God being Love, the oneness of humankind and the dignity of the body to be used for spiritual uplift and the immanence of God within, is a unique contribution in the spiritual history of India and justifies the encomium conferred on him by *Tāyumanavar* that he was the "*Emperor of Meditators*".

राग : हंसध्वनि Rāga : Hamsadhwani

1. तीयिनुं वेय्यन् पुनलिनुं तण्णियन्
आयिनुं ईशन् अरुळ् अऱिवारिल्लै
चेयिनुं नल्लन् अणियन् नल् अन्पार्क्कुत्
तायिनुं नल्लन् ताऴ्जटैयोने।

teeyinum veyyan punalinum taṇṇiyan
aayinum īśan aruḷ aṛivārillai
cheyinum nallan aṇiyan nal anpārkkut
taayinum nallan taazhajaṭaiyone.

1. Teeyinum Veyyan

He is more fiery than fire, cooler than the coolest lake,
Yet no one knows about the Lord's power!
He is as good as a child, He is the proximate one,
To those who love Him, He is as good as a mother!
The Lord with the matted hair!

राग : काम्बोजि

Rāga : Kamboji

2. चूट्टुवन् नेञ्जिटै वैप्पन् पिरान् एन्ऱु
पाटुवन् पन्मलर् तूविप्पणिन्तु निन्-
ऱाटुवन् आटि अमरर् पिरान् एन्ऱु
नाटुवन् यानिन् ऱऱिवतु ताने।

chooṭuvan nenjiṭai vaippan pirān enṛu
paaṭuvan panmalar toovippaṇintu nin-
raaṭuvan aaṭi amarar pirān enṛu
naaṭuvan yaanin ṛaṛivatu taane.

2. Chootuvan nenjitai

I will wear the Lord as my crown

I will keep Him in my heart!

Calling Him as my Lord, I will sing of His glories!

I will worship Him with many flowers!

I will dance and dance

and deeming Him the Chief of celestials,

I will seek refuge in Him.

राग : यमुनाकल्याणि Rāga : Yamunākalyāṇi

3. अन्पुं शिवमुं इरण्डेन्पर् अऱिविलार्
अन्पे शिवमावतु आरुं अऱिकिलार्
अन्पे शिवमावतु आरुं अऱिन्तपिन्
अन्पे शिवमाय् अमर्न्तिरुन्तारे।

anpum śivamum iraṇḍenpar aṛivilaar
anpe śivamaavatu aarum aṛikilaar
anpe śivamaavatu aaru aṛintapin
anpe śivamaay amarntiruntaare.

3. Anpum Sivamum

The ignorant say Love and God are different!

No one knows that Love is God!

After knowing that Love is God, (one realises)

God exists as love.

राग : शुद्ध धन्यासि Rāga : Śuddha Dhanyāsi

4. उळ्ळं पेरुङ्कोयिल् ऊनुडं पालयं
वळ्ळल् पिरानार्क्कु वाय् गोपुरवाशल्
तेळ्ळि त्तेळिवार्क्कु च्चीवन् शिवलिङ्गं
कळ्ळ प्पूलननन्तुं काळामणिविळक्के।

ul̤l̤am perunkoil ūnuḍam paalayam
val̤l̤al pirānaarkku vaay gopuravaaśal
tel̤l̤ittel̤ivaarkku cceevan śivalingam
kal̤l̤appulananantum kaal̤aamaṇivil̤akke.

4. Ullam perunkoil

The mind is a great temple, the fleshy body is a temple!
To the wise, the mouth is the temple tower gate!
To the clear minded, life is the idol of God!
The deceptive senses are the illuminating lamp!

राग : सहाना Rāga : Sahānā

5. पटमाट क्कोयिल् पकवर्कोन्रीयिल्
नटमाट क्कोयिल् नन्पर्क्कङ्काका
नटमाट क्कोयिल् नन्पर्क्कोन्रीयिल्
पटमाट क्कोयिल् पकवर्कतामे।

paṭamaaṭa kkoil pakavarkonreeyil
naṭamaaṭa kkoil nanparkkankaakaa
naṭamaaṭa kkoil nanparkkonreeyil
paṭamaaṭa kkoil pakavarkataame.

5. Padamātā koil

Gifts given to the Lord in the temple
do not reach the poor!
But gifts given to the poor
reach the Lord in the temple!

राग : रीतिगौळ Rāga : Rītigowḷa

6. वेदङ्कळाड मिकु आगममाडक्
गीतङ्कळाड किळरण्डं एऴाडप्
पूतङ्कलाड प्पुवनमुऴुताड
नातङ्कोण्डाटिनान् ज्ञानानन्दक्कूत्ते।

vedankaḷaaḍa miku aagamamaaḍag
geetankaḷaaḍa kiḷaraṇḍam ezhaaḍap
pootankalaaḍa ppuvanamuzhutaaḍa
naadankoṇḍāḍinān jnānānandakkootte.

6. Vedankalaada

When the Lord dances the dance of knowledge-bliss
accompanied by the *pranava* sound,
the Vedas dance, the varied scriptures dance!
Melodies dance! The seven worlds dance!
The elements dance! The entire cosmos dances!

राग : शंकराभरणं Rāga : Śankarābharaṇam

7. माणिक्कक्कूत्तनै वण्तिल्लैक्कूत्तनैप्
पूणुट्ट्र मन्रुळ् पुरिचडैक्कूत्तनैच्
चेणुट्ट्र चोतिच् चिवानन्दक्कूत्तनै
आणिप्पोर् कूत्तनै यारुरैप्पारे।

maaṇikkakkoottanai vaṇtillaikkoottanaip
pooṇuṭṭramanruḷ purijaḍaikkoottanaic
ceṇuṭṭra coticcivaananda kkoottanai
aaṇippoṛ koottanai yaaruraippaare.

7. Maaṇikkakkoottanai

Who can describe
the jewel of a dancer, who dances in Tillai,
the dancer with the matted locks,
that distant divine Light who dances in auspicious bliss,
the golden dancer who is the support of this universe.

राग : मोहनं Rāga : Mohanam

8. आडिय कालुं अतिरूचिलम्पोशैयुं
पाडिय पाट्टुं पलवान नट्टमुं
कूडिय कोलं गुरुपरन् कोण्डाडत्
तेडियुळेकण्डु तीर्न्तट्ट्रवारे।

aaḍiya kaalum atircilamposaiyum
paaḍiya paaṭṭum palavaana naṭṭamum
kooḍiya kolam guruparan koṇḍaaḍat
teḍiyuḷekaṇḍu teerntaṭṭṛavaare.

8. Aadiyakaalum

The dancing legs with their jingling anklets,
accompanied by the songs sung and the various poses!
the beautiful spectacle of the dancing Lord!
I saw within my heart,
ending this cycle of births and deaths!

राग : सिन्धुभैरवि Rāga : Sindhubhairavi

9. उणर्वुं अवने उयिरुं अवने
पुणरुं अवने पुलवि अवने
इणरुं अवन्तन्नै एण्णलुं आकान्
तुणरुं मलर्क्कन्द त्तुळ्ळिनिन्ऱाने।

uṇarvum avane uyirum avane
puṇarum avane pulavi avane
iṇarum avantannai eṇṇalum aakaan
tuṇarum malarkkandattuḷḷininraane.

9. Uṇarvum avane

He is consciousness!
He is life!
He is union!
He is separation!
He is continuity!
He transcends thought!
He is the fragrance in the flower within!

राग : मध्यमावति Rāga : Madhyamāvati

10. निऱं पल एव्वण्णं अव्वण्णं ईशन्
अऱं पल एव्वण्णं अव्वण्णं इन्पं
मऱं पल एव्वण्णं अव्वण्णं पावं
पुऱं पल काणिनुं पोट्ट्रकिलारे।

niṛam pala evvaṇṇam avvaṇṇam īśan
aṛam pala evvaṇṇam avvaṇṇam inpam
maṛam pala evvaṇṇam avvaṇṇam paavam
puṛam pala kaaṇinum poṭṭrakilaare.

10. Niram pala evvannam

Colours are many. So is the Lord (multicoloured)
Virtues are many. So are the facets of His bliss!
Vices are varied; so are His inequities!
Though we may see many external forms,
adore Him who is immanent in all this variety!

SONGS OF KALIDASA

Song	*Raga*
1. Vedanteshu yamahurekapurusham	Yaman
2. Ya srstih srashturadya	Hamsadhwani
3. Ekaisvarye sthitopi	Kanada
4. *Syamaladandakam*	*Ragamalika*
Manikyaveenam	Poorvikalyani
Mātā marakatasyama	Yamunakalyani
Sadarārabdha	Ritigowla
Charu gorochana	Suruti
Divyahalamadodvela	Desh
Mugdhamandasmitodara	Sahana
Sulalitanava	Kanada
Vasararambhavela	Abheri
Tarakarajinikasa	Sri
Charusinchat	Suddhadhanyasi
Vikasita navakimsukatamra	Kapi
Prahvadevesa	Todi
Suruchira navaratnapithasthite	Sindhubhairavi
Saravanaharana	Hindolam
Panipadma dvayena	Suddhasaveri
Sarva teerthatmike	Madhyamavati
5. *Navaratnamala*	*Ragamalika*
	(Yaman, Hamsa-dhwani, Kanada, Suruti, Mohanam, Desh, Khamas, Ritigowla, Madhyamavati)

KALIDASA

KALIDASA (6th Century A.D.)

Kalidasa is the national poet of India and the greatest Sanskrit poet.

He is to Sanskrit literature what William Shakespeare is to English literature.

Kalidasa has composed the lyrics: *Ritusamhāra* and *Meghadūta*, the two epics: *Raghuvamsa* and *Kumārasambhava*, and the three plays: *Malavikagnimitra*, *Vikramorvaśiya* and *Śākuntalam.*

How does this romantic poet find a place among the mystic saints of India, is a question which can legitimately be raised.

The answer is contained in Kalidasa's own dictum: "*Nanṛshi kurute kāvyam*": "One who is not a sage cannot create a poem."

Though Kalidasa dealt with the sensory emotions of princes and princesses and celestial beings, there is no denying the fact that he was an ardent devotee of God, whom he worshipped as the Primordial Father-Mother.

The benedictory verses at the beginning of his works (included in this volume) bring out his ardent devotion to God.

The legend about his transformation from a dumb shepherd to a proliferous poet by the grace of the Divine Mother is too wellknown to merit repetition. The composition *Symālādandakam* (included in this compendium) is his homage in gratitude.

The sensual imagery used by Kalidasa in spiritual devotion is not uncommon among the mystics of India. Jayadeva, Vidyapati and even Sankaracharya have used this in their devotional songs.

राग : यमन Rāga : Yaman

1. वेदान्तेषु यमाहुरेकपुरुषं व्याप्य स्थितं रोदसी
यस्मिन्नीश्वर इतनन्यविषय शब्दो यथार्थाक्षरः।
अन्तर्यश्च मुमुक्षुभिर्नियमितप्राणादिभिर्मृग्यते
स स्थाणुः स्थिरभक्तियोगसुलभो निःश्रेयसायास्तु वः॥

(विक्रमोर्वशीयम्)

vedānteshu yamaahurekapurusham vyaapya sthitam rodasī
yasminnīśvara itananyavishaya śabdo yathārthāksharaḥ
antaryaśca mumukshubhirniyamitaprāṇādibhirmṛgyate
sa sthāṇuḥ sthirabhaktiyogasulabho niḥśreyasāyaastu vaḥ.

(Vikramorvaśīyam)

1. Vedanteshu yamahurekapurusham

He, who is mentioned in the *Upanishads* as the unique Person,

who remains, pervading heaven and earth,

with reference to whom, the word *Īśvara*, the Supreme Ruler, not applicable to anyone else, finds its true meaning,

who is sought after, in the inner recesses of their hearts, by those desiring liberation, through control of breath etc.

That permanent One,

who is easily attained through the yoga of unflinching devotion,

Let Him grant the supreme beatitude to you!

राग : हंसध्वनि Rāga : Hamsadhwani

2. या सृष्टिः स्त्रष्टुराद्या वहति विधिहुतं या हविर्या च होत्री
ये द्वे कालं विधत्तः श्रुतिविषयगुणा या स्थिता व्याप्य विश्वम्।
यामाहुः सर्वबीजप्रकृतिरिति यया प्राणिनः प्राणवन्तः
प्रत्यक्षाभिः प्रपन्नस्तनुभिरवतु वस्ताभिरष्टाभिरीशः॥

(शाकुन्तलम्)

yaa sṛshṭiḥ srashṭuraadyaa vahati vidhihutam yaa haviryaa ca hotree

ye dve kaalam vidhattaḥ śrutivishayaguṇā yā sthitaa vyāpya viśvam

yaamaahuḥ sarvabeejaprakṛtiriti yayaa praaṇinaḥ praaṇavantaḥ

pratyakshaabhiḥ prapannastanubhiravatu vastaabhirashṭaabhirīśaḥ.

(Śākuntalam)

2. Ya sṛṣṭih srasturādya

May the Supreme Lord protect you through these eight patent forms of His:

That which is the first creation of the Creator,

That which bears the offering made according to scriptural rites,

That one who makes the offering,
Those two who make time,

Those qualities which are perceived by the ears,
That which pervades the universe,

That primordial Nature which is the seed of all beings

That by which all living beings breathe.

राग : कानडा Rāga : Kānaḍā

3. एकैश्वर्ये स्थितोऽपि प्रणतबहुफले यः स्वयं कृत्तिवासाः
कान्तासंमिश्रदेहोऽप्यविषयमनसां यः परस्ताद्यतीनाम्।
अष्टाभिर्यस्य कृत्स्नं जगदपि तनुभिर्बिभ्रतो नाभिमानः
सन्मार्गालोकनाय व्यपनयतु स वस्तामसीं वृत्तिमीशः॥

(मालविकाग्निमित्रम्)

ekaiśvarye sthitoapi praṇatabahuphale yaḥ svayam kṛttivāsāḥ

kaantaasammiśradehoapyavishayamanasaam yaḥ parastaadyatīnām

ashṭaabhiryasya kṛtsnam jagadapi tanubhirbibhrato nābhimānaḥ

sanmargaalokanaaya vyapanayatu sa vastaamaseem vṛttimīśaḥ.

(Malavikagnimitram)

3. Ekaiśvarye sthitoapi

Though He remains in unique supremacy and grants many fruitful results to those who bow to Him, He himself wears only an elephant skin!
Though His body is ever united with His spouse, He is yet superior to those sages whose minds are averse to sensory pleasures,
Though He controls the whole universe through His eight forms, He does not have any arrogance,
May that Auspicious Lord Siva
dispel your state of dark ignorance to enable you to see the righteous path!

4. श्यामला-दण्डकम्

राग : पूर्वि कल्याणि Rāga : Poorvi Kalyāṇi

माणिक्यवीणां उपलालयन्तीं
मदालसां मञ्जुल वाग्विलासां।
माहेन्द्रनील द्युति कोमलाङ्गीं
मातङ्गकन्यां मनसा स्मरामि॥

चतुर्भुजे चन्द्रकलावतंसे कुचोन्नते कुङ्कुमरागशोणे।
पुण्ड्रेक्षु पाशाङ्कुश पुष्पबाण हस्ते नमस्ते जगतेकमातः॥

maaṇikyaveeṇaam upalaalayanteem
madaalasaam manjula vaagvilaasaam
maahendraneela dyuti komalāngeem
mātangakanyaam manasaa smarāami.

caturbhuje candrakalāvatamse kuconnate
kumkumarāgaśoṇe

puṇḍrekshu paaśaankuśa pushpabaaṇa haste
namaste jagatekamaataḥ.

4. Śyāmalā-Daṇḍakam

Māṇikyaveenam

I meditate in my mind on the daughter of Matanga,
who plays with the bejewelled lute,
is youthful and speaks soft words,
whose limbs are beautiful and radiant like Indra's blue sapphire.

O! Mother of the world! Prostrations to You!
who are four-armed and wear the crescent moon in your crest,
whose breasts are high and whose body is crimson hued like vermilion!
and who hold sugarcane, noose, goad and the flower arrow in your hands.

राग : यमुना कल्याणि — Rāga : Yamunā Kalyāṇi

माता मरकतश्यामा मातङ्गी मदशालिनी।
कटाक्षयतु कल्याणी कदम्बवनवासिनी॥

जय मातङ्गतनये! जयनीलोत्पलद्युते।
जय सङ्गीतरसिके जय लीलाशुकप्रिये॥
जय जननी! सुधा समुद्रान्त हृद्यन् मणिद्वीप संरूढ़
बिल्वाटवी मध्य कल्पद्रुमाकल्प कादम्ब कान्तार वासप्रिये।
कृत्तिवासप्रिये! सर्वलोकप्रिये॥

mātā marakataśyāmā mātangī madaśālinī
kaṭākshayatu kalyāṇī kadambavanavāsinī.

jaya mātangatanaye! jayaneelotpaladyute!
jaya sangeetarasike jaya leelaaśukapriye!
jaya jananī! sudhaa samudraanta hṛdyan maṇidveepa samrūḍha
bilvāṭavee madhya kalpadrumākalpa kādamba kāntāra vāsapriye!
kṛttivāsapriye! sarvalokapriye!

Mātā marakataśyāma

May the mother, who is green-hued like the green emerald,

the youthful daughter of Sage Matanga,

the auspicious One who lives in the kadamba forest

bestow her glance of grace on us.

Hail O daughter of Matanga!

Hail O goddess radiant like the blue lotus!

Hail O Connoisseuse of music!

Hail O Mother fond of sporting with the parrot!

Hail O Mother!

O universally adored Mother! O Beloved of Siva,

who wears the elephant skin!

Hail O Mother, who love to live in the *Kadamba* forest,

with the *Kalpa* tree, in the midst of *Bilwa* trees located

in the island of *Manidwipa,* in the centre of the ambrosial

ocean!

राग : रीतिगौळ Rāga : Rītigowḷa

साधरारब्ध सङ्गीत सम्भावना सम्भ्रमालोल नीप-
स्रगाबद्ध चुली सनाथत्रिके, सानुमत्पुत्रिके! शेखरी भूत
शीतांशुरेखा मयूखावलीबद्ध सुस्निग्ध नीलालक श्रेणि
श्रृङ्गारिते! लोक सम्भाविते! कामलीला धनुः सन्निभ
भ्रूलतापुष्प सन्दोह सन्देह कृल्लोचने! वाक् सुधा सेचने!

saadharaarabdha sangeeta sambhaavanaa
sambhramālola neepa-
sragaabaddha culī sanaathatrike, saanumatputrike!
śekharee bhūta śeetaamśurekhaa mayukhaavalībaddha
susnigdha neelaalaka śreṇiśṛngārite! loka sambhaavite!
kaamaleelaa dhanuḥ sannibhabhroolataapushpa
sandoha sandeha kṛllocane! vaaksudhaa secane!

Sādarārabdha

O daughter of Himavan!
when you enjoy the music just begun,
your hair dances and the flowers in them
shake and make your back beautiful.
O Mother venerated by all the worlds!
Your forehead is adorned by the dark hair falling along
with the rays of the moon in your crest!
O Mother who speak words sweet as nectar!
Your eyes look as if they are the flowers which have
bloomed on the creepers of your eyebrows which are
curved like the bow of Cupid!

राग : सुरुटि Rāga : Suruṭi

चारु गोरोचनापङ्क केली ललामाभिरामे सुरामे! रमे!।
प्रोल्लसत् वालिका मौक्तिक श्रेणिका चन्द्रिका मण्डलोद्-
भासि लावण्य गण्डस्थलन्यस्त कस्तूरिका पत्ररेखा समुद्भूत
सौरभ्य सम्भ्रान्त भृङ्गाङ्गना गीत सान्द्री भवन् मन्त्र
तन्त्रीश्वरे! सुस्वरे! भास्वरे! वल्लकी वादन प्रक्रिया-
लोल ताळी दळाबद्ध ताटङ्क भूषा विशेषान्विते! सिद्ध
सम्मानिते!

caaru gorocanaapanka keleelalaamaabhiraame suraame! rame!

prollasat vaalikaa mauktika śrenikaa candrikaa

maṇḍalod bhaasi laavaṇya gaṇḍasthalanyasta

kastūrikaa patrarekhaa samudbhūta saurabhya

sambhraanta bhṛngaanganaageeta saandrī bhavan mantra

tantrīśvare! susvare! bhāsvare! vallakīvaadana

prakriyaalola taaḷee daḷaabaddha tāṭanka

bhūshaaviśeshānvite! siddhasammaanite!

Cāru gorocanāpanka

O Divine beauty who steal hearts!

You wear the auspicious mark on your forehead, made

of *gorochana*, exuding fragrance and loveliness.

O Radiant One! who have an auspicious voice!

who lord over all mantras and tantras!

The effulgent pearls set in your ear ornaments cast their

light on your cheeks!

The fragrance of the *Kasturi* marks painted on them

attracts the bees, whose humming sound resembles

the music of your lute

O goddess venerated by *Siddhas*!*

You shine by your shaking ear ornaments made of palm

leaf when you sway your head, while playing the lute!

*Evolved sages.

राग : देश Rāga : Desh

दिव्य हाला मदोद्वेल हेला लसत् चक्षु-
रान्दोलन श्री समाक्षिप्त कर्णैक नीलोत्पले! श्यामले! पूरिताशेष
लोकाभिवाञ्छा फले निर्मले! श्री फले!। स्वेद बिन्दूल्लसत् फाल
लावण्य निष्यन्द सन्दोह सन्देह कृन्नासिका मौक्तिके!
सर्वमन्त्रात्मिके सर्व विश्वात्मिके! कालिके!

divyahaalaa madodvelahelaa lasat cakshu-
raandolana śrī samaakshipta karṇaika neelotpale! śyāmale!
pooritaaśesha lokaabhivaanchaaphale nirmale! śree phale! sveda
bindūllasat phaalalaavaṇya nishyanda sandoha sandeha kṛnnāsikaa
mauktike! sarvamantrātmike sarva viśvātmike! kālike!

Divya hala madodvela

O stainless One! O dark-hued goddess, Syamala!
Who bestow auspicious fruits!
Who fulfil all the desires of people!
The loveliness of your eyes outrivals the beauty of the blue lotuses you wear above your ears!
O dark goddess!
You are the soul of the universe!
You are the soul of all mantras!
The sweat drops on your forehead which make your forehead beautiful
Look like the reflection of the pearls in your nose ornament!

राग : सहाना Rāga : Sahānā

मुग्ध मन्दस्मितोदार वक्त्र स्फुरत्पूग ताम्बूल कर्पूर कण्ठोत्करे!
ज्ञान मुद्राकरे! सर्व सम्पत्करे! पद्म भास्वत्करे! श्रीकरे!
कुन्द पुष्प द्युति स्निग्ध दन्तावली निर्मलालोल कल्लोल
सम्मेलनस्मेर शोणाधरे! चारुवीणाधरे! पक्वबिम्बाधरे!

mugdha mandasmitodaara vaktra sphuratpūga
tāmboola karpūra kaṇṭhotkare! jnānamudrākare!
sarva sampatkare! padmabhāsvatkare! śrīkare!
kunda pushpa dyuti snigdha dantāvalee nirmalaalola
kallola sammelanasmera śoṇādhare! cāruveeṇaadhare!
pakvabimbādhare!

Mugdha mandasmitodara

O goddess who create auspicious welfare!
You bestow all forms of wealth!
Your hands shine like lotuses! They indicate the way to knowledge!
Your face shines with your mouth reddened by the *tamboola* comprising camphor, arecanut, etc.
and wreathed in smiles.
O goddess who carry the lute in your hands
and have lips red like the ripe *Bimba* fruit!
The row of your teeth, pure white like jasmine buds,
along with your smile heighten the beauty of your lips.

राग : कानडा Rāga : Kānaḍā

सुललित नव यौवनारम्भ चन्द्रोदयोद्वेल लावण्य
दुग्धार्णवाविर्भवत् कम्बु बिम्वोक भृत्कन्धरे सत्कला
मन्दिरे मन्थरे! दिव्य रत्न प्रभा बन्धुरच्छन्न हारादि
भूषा समुद्योतमानानवद्यांशु शोभे! शुभे!। रत्न केयूर
रश्मिच्छठापल्लव प्रोल्लसत् दोर्लता राजिते! योगिभिः
पूजिते! विश्व दिङ्मण्डलव्यापि माणिक्य तेजस्फुरत्
कङ्कणालङ्कृते विभ्रमालङ्कृते साधुभिस् सत्कृते!

sulalita nava yauvanaarambha candrodayodvela lāvaṇya
dugdhārṇavaavirbhavat kambu bimboka bhṛtkandhare satkalaa
mandire manthare! divya ratna prabhaa bandhuracchanna hāraadi
bhūshaa samudyotamaanaanavadyaamśu śobhe! śubhe! ratna keyūra
raśmicchaṭhaapallava prollasat dorlataa raajite! yogibhiḥ
pūjite! viśva dingmaṇḍalavyaapi maaṇikya tejasphurat
kankaṇaalankṛte vibhramaalankṛte saadhubhis satkṛte!

Sulalita nava

Your neck is like the conch which rose out of the ambrosial ocean rendered lovely by the rays of the rising

moon.

O Temple of all fine arts!

O goddess devoid of discrimination!

Your faultless limbs are radiant with the pure diamond

and pearl necklaces which adorn your body!

O Auspicious One!

Your hands which resemble creepers radiate effulgence

due to the armlets studded with jewels!

O goddess worshipped by Yogis!

You are adorned by the bangles studded with

diamonds whose radiance spreads to the four quarters!

You shine by your sports!

You are venerated by the sages!

राग : आभेरि Rāga : Ābheri

वासरारम्भवेला समृज्जृम्भमाणारविन्द प्रतिद्वन्द्वि पाणिद्वये
सन्ततोद्यद्वये अद्वये! दिव्य रत्नोर्मिका दीधितिस्तोम
सन्ध्यायमानाङ्गुली पल्लवोद्यन्नखेन्दु प्रभा मण्डले
सन्नुताखण्डले! चित्प्रभा मण्डले प्रोल्लसत् कुण्डले!

vaasaraarambhavelaa samṛjjṛmbhamaaṇaaravinda pratidvandvi pāṇidvaye

santatodyadvaye advaye! divya ratnormikaa deedhitistoma

sandhyaayamaanaanggulee pallavodyannakhendu prabhā maṇḍale

sannutaakhaṇḍale! citprabhaa maṇḍale prollasat kuṇḍale!

Vāsarārambha

You have two hands which are like lotuses which bloom at dawn!

You ever show mercy!

You are the One without a second!

The gems on the rings worn on your fingers resemble the evening glow of the sun!

Your moon-like nails add to your beauty!

You manifest as consciousness!

You wear shining ear ornaments!

You are worshipped by Indra!

राग : श्री Rāga : Śrī

तारका राजि नीकाश हारावलि स्मेर चारुस्तनाभोग
भारा नमन्मध्यवल्ली वलिच्छेद वीची समुल्लास सन्दर्शि-
ताकार सौन्दर्य रत्नाकरे वल्लकी भृत्करे किङ्कर श्रीकरे!
हेम कुम्भोपमोत्तुङ्ग वक्षोज भारावनम्रे त्रिलोकावनम्रे!
लसत् वृत्त गम्भीर नाभी सरस्तीर शैबाल शङ्काकरश्याम-
रोमावली भूषणे मञ्जु सम्भाषणे!

tarakaa raaji neekaaśa haaraavali smera chaarustanaabhoga

bhaaraa namanmadhyavallee valiccheda veecī samullaasa

sandarśitaakaara saundarya ratnaakare vallakī bhṛtkare kimkaraśrīkare!

hema kumbhopamottunga vakshojabhaaraavanamre trilokāvanamre!

lasat vṛtta gambhīra naabhee sarasteera śaibāla śankaakaraśyāma

romāvalī bhūshaṇe manju sambhāshaṇe!

Tarakā rāji

O goddess who hold the lute!

You are the treasurehouse of beauty!

You create prosperity for your devotees!

Your weighty breasts are rendered beautiful by the necklace of pearls which resemble stars in the night sky!

The line of dark hair which rises from your deep navel resembles the plant which grows on the banks of ponds.

O goddess who speak softly!

राग : शुद्ध धन्यासि Rāga : Śuddha Dhanyāsi

चारु शिञ्जत् कटीसूत्र
निर्भर्त्सित अनङ्ग लीला धनुः शिञ्जिनीडम्बरे! दिव्य-
रत्नांबरे! पद्म रागोल्लसन्मेखला भास्वर श्रोणि
शोभाजित स्वर्ण भूभृत्तले चन्द्रिकाशीतले!

chaaru śinjat kaṭee sūtra
nirbhartsita ananga leelaa dhanuḥ śinjineeḍambare! divya-
ratnaambare! padma raagollasanmekhalaa bhaasvara śroṇi
śobhaajita svarṇa bhūbhṛttale candrikaa śeetale!

Cārucincat

Your beautiful waist belt making soft sounds outrivals
the glory of Cupid's bow!
You wear a bejewelled garment!
You are cool like the moon!
The beauty of the coral studded waist belt outrivals
the beauty of the golden peak of Mount Meru!

राग : कापि Rāga : Kāpi

विकसित नवकिंशुकाताम्र दिव्यांशुकच्छन्न चारु
शोभा पराभूत सिन्दूर शोणायमानेन्द्रमातङ्ग हस्तार्गले
वैभवानर्गले श्यामले! कोमल स्निग्ध नीलोत्पलोद्भासिता
नङ्ग तूणीर शङ्काकरोदार जङ्घालते! चारु लीलागते!
नम्र दिग्पाल सीमन्तिनी कुन्तल स्निग्ध नील प्रभा पुञ्ज
सञ्जात दूर्वाङ्कुराशङ्क सारङ्ग संयोग रिङ्खन्नखेन्दूज्वले
प्रोज्ज्वले! निर्मले!

vikasita navakimśukaataamra divyāmśukacchanna caaru
śobhaa paraabhūta sindūra śoṇaayamaanendramaatanga hastaargale!
vaibhavaanargale śyāmale! komala snigdha neelotpalodbhaasitaa
nanga tūṇeera śankaakarodaara jangghaalate! caaru leelāgate!
namra digpāla seemantinī kuntala snigdha neela prabhā punja
sanjaata dūrvaankuraaśanka saaranga samyoga rinkhannakhendujvale
projjvale! nirmale!

Vikasita

O goddess *Syaamala,* dark-hued One!
You exude divine radiance!
You wear a silken garment which resembles the full blown *Kimsuka** flower!
Your lovely legs resembling blue lotuses look like Cupid's quiver!
You have beautiful steps!
Your nails entwined with the hair of bowing spouses of the Guardians of quarters resemble kusa grass and disappoint the deer who come to eat them.
They shine like the shadowless moon!
O pure, stainless One!

---

*Hibiscus flower.

राग : तोडि Rāga : Toḍi

प्रह्व देवेश लक्ष्मीश भूतेश दैत्येशयक्षेश
वागीश कीनाश तोयेश वायु अग्नि कोटीर माणिक्य
सङ्धृष्ट बालातपोद्दाम लाक्षारसारुण्य तारुण्य लक्ष्मी
गृहीताङ्घ्रि पद्मे सुपद्मे! उमे!

prahva deveśa lakshmīśa bhūteśa daityeśayaksheśa
vaageeśa keenaaśa toyeśa vāyu agni koṭeera maaṇikya
sangdhṛshṭa baalaatapoddaama laakshaarasaaruṇya tāruṇya lakshmī
gṛhītaanghri padme supadme! ume!

Prahva devesa

O goddess who look like the lotus! O *Uma*!
Your lotus-like feet shine like the crimson sun,
because of the jewels in the crowns of
Indra, Visnu, Siva, Varuna, Brahma, Yama, Kubera,
Wind, Fire deities and others
who bow at your feet.

राग : सिन्धु भैरवि

Rāga : Sindhu Bhairavi

सुरुचिर नवरत्नपीठस्थिते! सुस्थिते! रत्न सिंहासने रत्न पद्मासने शङ्क
पद्म द्वयोपाश्रिते! तत्र विघ्नेश दूर्वावटु क्षेत्रपालैर्युते! मत्तमातङ्ग कन्या
समूहान्विते मञ्जुला मेनकाद्यङ्गना मानिते! भैरवैरष्टभिर्वेष्टिते!
देवि वामादिभिः संश्रिते शक्तिभिः सेविते! धात्रि लक्ष्म्यादि
शक्त्यष्टकैः सम्युते! मातृका मण्डलैर्मण्डिते! पञ्चबाणात्मिके
पञ्चबाणेन रत्या च सम्भाविते! प्रीति भाजा वसन्तेन च
आनन्दिते! भक्ति भाजां परं श्रेयसे! कल्पसे योगिनां मानसे
द्योतसे च्छन्दसामोजसा भ्राजसे! गीत विद्या विनोदाति
तृष्णेन कृष्णेन सम्पूज्यसे! भक्तिमत् चेतसा वेधसा स्तूयसे!
विश्व हृद्येन वाद्येन विद्याधरैर्गीयसे!

surucira navaratnapeeṭhasthite! susthite! ratna simhāsane ratna padmāsane
śankapadmadvayopāśrite! tatra vighneśa dūrvaavaṭu kshetrapaalairyute! mattamātanga kanyaa
samūhaanvite manjulā menakaadyanganaa manite! bhairavairashṭabhirveshṭite!
devi vāmādibhiḥ samśrite śaktibhiḥ sevite! dhaatri lakshmyādi
śaktyashṭakaiḥ samyute! mātṛkaa maṇḍalairmaṇḍite! pancabāṇātmike
pancabāṇena ratyā ca sambhāvite! preetibhājaa vasantena ca
ānandite! bhakti bhājām param śreyase! kalpase yoginām mānase
dyotase cchandasāmojasaa bhrājase! gītavidyā vinodāti
tṛshṇena kṛshṇena sampūjyase! bhaktimat cetasā vedhasā
stūyase! viśvahṛdyena vādyena vidyādharairgīyase!

Suruchira

You are seated on the attractive throne set with the nine

types of gems!

You are well seated!

In the diamond throne, in the lotus pose, you are

accompanied by the conch and the lotus!

You are with Ganesa and other guardians of quarters!

Groups of wild elephants surround you!

Beautiful damsels like *Menaka* eulogise you!

The eight Bhairavas salute you!

You are served by the various powers!

O Protectress! You are accompanied by the eight Lakshmis!

You are with groups of *Mātrikas*!*

You are the soul of the god of love!

You are worshipped by Cupid and his wife Rati!

You are delighted by pleasing spring!

You lift up your devotees!

You shine in the minds of Yogis!

You shine in all the universal rhythms!

You are worshipped by Krishna who is eager to teach the

gospel of Gita!

Devoted minds praise you! *Vidyādharas** sing of you with universally attractive music.

*Semi-divine beings.

राग : हिन्दोलं Rāga : Hindolam

श्रवण हरण दक्षिण क्वाणया वीणया किन्नरै-
र्गीयसे ! यक्ष गन्धर्व सिद्धाङ्गना मण्डलैरर्च्यसे ! सर्व
सौभाग्य वाञ्छावतीभिः वधूभिः सुराणां समाराध्यसे !
सर्व विद्या विशेषात्मकं चाटु गाथा समुच्चाटनं कण्ठ-
मूलोल्लसत् वर्णराजित्रयं ! कोमलं श्यामलोदार पक्षद्वयं
तुण्ड शोभातिदूरी भवत् किंशुकं तं शुकं लालयन्ती
परिक्रीडसे !

śravaṇa haraṇa dakshiṇa kvāṇayaa veeṇayaa kinnarair-
geeyase! yaksha gandharva siddhānganaa maṇḍalairarcyase!
sarva saubhāgya vānchāvatībhiḥ vadhūbhiḥ surāṇām samārādhyase!
sarva vidyā viśeshaatmakam chaaṭu gaathaa samuccaaṭanam kaṇṭha-
mūlollasat varṇarājitrayam! komalam śyāmalodāra pakshadvayam
tuṇḍa śobhātidūrī bhavat kimśukam tam śukam lālayantī
parikreeḍase!

Śravaṇa haraṇa

Your glory is sung by *Kinnaras,* the celestial singers accompanied by the music emanating from their lutes which steals the ears!

You are worshipped by *Yakshas, Gandharvas* and groups of celestial beauties.

You are meditated upon by the brides of angels who desire auspicious good fortune!

Three lines adorn your neck, which is the source of beautiful poems and the essence of all specialised learning!

Your two sides dark-hued and outrivalling the *Kimsuka* flower are lovely,

You play with your parrot fondling them.

राग : शुद्ध सावेरि Rāga : Śuddha Sāveri

पाणिपद्म द्वयेनाक्षमालामपि स्फाटिकीं
ज्ञानसारात्मकं पुस्तकं च अङ्कुशं पाशमाबिभ्रती येन
सञ्चिन्त्यसे तस्य वक्त्रान्तरात् गद्य पद्यात्मिका भारती
निस्सरेत्! येन वा यावका माकृतिः भाव्यसे! तस्य
वश्या भवन्ति स्त्रियः पुरुषाः। येन वा शातकुम्भ द्युतिः
भाव्यसे! सोऽपि लक्ष्मी सहस्रैः परिक्रीडते! किं न
सिद्ध्येद्वपुः श्यामलं कोमलं चन्द्रचूडान्वितं तावकं
ध्यायतः। तस्य लीला सरोवारिधिः तस्य केलीवनं
नन्दनं, तस्य भद्रासनं भूतलं, तस्य गीर्देवता किङ्करी, तस्य
च आज्ञाकरी श्रीः स्वयं॥

pāṇipadma dvayenaakshamaalaamapi sphāṭikeem
jnānasārātmakam pustakam ca ankuśam
pāśamābibhratī yena
samcintyase tasya vaktrāntarāt gadya padyātmikā
bhāratī
nissaret! yena vā yāvakā mākṛtiḥ bhāvyase! tasya
vaśyā bhavanti striyaḥ purushāḥ. yena vā śātakumbha
dyutiḥ
bhāvyase! soapi lakshmī sahasraiḥ parikreeḍate! kim na
siddhyedvapuḥ śyāmalam komalam candracooḍānvitam
tāvakam
dhyāyataḥ. tasya leelaa sarovāridhiḥ, tasya kelīvanam
nandanam, tasya bhadrāsanam bhūtalam,
tasya geerdevataa
kimkaree, tasya ca ājnākarī śrīḥ svayam.

Pāṇipadma dvayena

He who thinks of the goddess
who holds in her two lotus-like hands
the garland of crystal beads, the book which is the
essence of all knowledge, the goad and the noose,
from his mouth, the goddess of learning will cause
prose and poetry to flow!
He who meditates on such a form (of the goddess)
will find men and women attracted to him.
He who meditates on her golden radiance
will sport with thousands of riches,
What will he not get,
who meditates on your dark, lovely, crescent-crested
form?
The oceans will become his sporting lakes!
The heavenly garden will become his sporting ground!
The earth will become his throne!
The goddess of learning will be his obedient servant
and the goddess of riches will carry out his commands!

राग : मध्यमावति | Rāga : Madhyamāvati

सर्व तीर्थात्मिके! सर्व मन्त्रात्मिके! सर्व
तन्त्रात्मिके! सर्व यन्त्रात्मिके! सर्व पीठात्मिके! सर्वतत्वा-
त्मिके सर्व शक्त्यात्मिके! सर्व विद्यात्मिके! सर्व योगात्मिके!
सर्व नादात्मिके! सर्व शब्दात्मिके! सर्व विश्वात्मिके! सर्व
दीक्षात्मिके! सर्व सर्वात्मिके! सर्वगे हे जगन्मातृगे पाहि मां
पाहि मां पाहि मां देवि! तुभ्यं नमो देवि तुभ्यं नमो
देवि तुभ्यं नमः॥

sarva teerthātmike! sarva mantrātmike! sarva
tantrātmike! sarva yantrātmike! sarva peeṭhaatmike!
sarvatatvātmike sarva śaktyātmike! sarva vidyātmike!
sarva yogātmike! sarva nādātmike! sarva śabdātmike!
sarva viśvātmike! sarva deekshātmike! sarva sarvātmike!
sarvage he jaganmātṛge pāhi mām
pāhi mām pāhi mām devi! tubhyam namo devi tubhyam
namo devi tubhyam namaḥ.

Sarva teerthatmike

O goddess who are the soul of all holy rivers!
You are the soul of all Mantras!
You are the soul of all Tantras!
You are the soul of all Yantras!
You are the soul of all holy seats!
You are the soul of all truths!
You are the soul of all strengths!
You are the soul of all learning!
You are the soul of all yogas!
You are the soul of all sounds!
You are the soul of all voices!
You are the soul of the entire cosmos!
You are the soul of all observances!
You are the soul of everything!
O Mother of the universe who pervade everything!
Protect me! Protect me! Protect me!
Prostrations to you!
Prostrations to you!
Prostrations to you!

5. नवरत्नमाला

राग : यमन Rāga : Yaman

1. ओङ्कार पञ्जर शुकीं उपनिषदुद्यानकेलिकलकण्ठीं
आगम विपिन मयूरीं आर्यां अन्तर्विभावये गौरीं ॥

omkāra pancara śukīm
upanishadudyānakelikalakaṇṭhīm
āgama vipina mayūrīm āryām antarvibhāvaye gaurīm.

राग : हंसध्वनि Rāga : Hamsadhwani

2. दयमान दीर्घनयनां देशिकरुपेण दर्शिताभ्युदयां
वामकुचनिहितवीणां वरदां संङ्गीतमातृकां वन्दे ॥

dayamāna dīrghanayanām deśikarupeṇa
darśitābhyudayām
vāmakucanihitavīṇām varadām sangītamātṛkām
vande.

5. Navaratnamālā

1. Omkara pancara sukim

I meditate in my mind on the noble, fair goddess,
who is like the parrot in the cage of the Pranava sound, AUM,
is like the cuckoo in the garden of Upanishads,
and is like the peacock in the forest of the Vedas.

2. Dayamāna dīrghanayanam

I bow to the mother of music,
who ever gives boons,
who has long compassionate eyes,
who, as a spiritual teacher, shows the way to welfare,
and who bears the lute on her left breast.

राग : कानडा Rāga : Kānaḍā

3. श्यामालिम सौकुमार्यां सौन्दर्यानन्द सम्पदुन्मेषां
तरुणिम करुणापूरां मदजन कल्लोल लोचनां वन्दे॥

śyāmālima saukumāryām saundaryānanda sampadunmeshām
taruṇima karuṇāpūrām madajana kallolalocanām vande.

राग : सुरुटि Rāga : Suruṭi

4. नखमुख सुस्वरित वीणां नादरसास्वादनवनवोल्लासां
मुख मम्ब मोदयतु मां मुग्धाताडङ्ग मुग्धहसितं ते॥

nakhamukha susvarita vīṇām nādarasāsvādanavanavollāsām
mukhamamba modayatu mām mugdhātāḍanga mugdhahasitam te.

3. Syāmālima saukumaryam

I worship the goddess,
who has the loveliness of the black cuckoo,
who is cheerful with her wealth of beauty and bliss,
who has eyes which are full of compassion towards the young and inimical towards arrogant persons.

4. Nakhamukha

O Mother! Let your face make me happy,
which has the beautiful earrings and a lovely smile,
and which enjoys the ever new notes produced
in the lute played with your nailtips.

राग : मोहनं Rāga : Mohanam

5. सरिगमपधनिरतां तां वीणासंक्रान्तकान्त हस्तां तां
शान्तां मृदुलस्वान्तां कुचभरतां तां नमामि शिवकान्तां॥

sarigamapadhaniratām tām vīṇāsamkrāntakānta hastām tām
śāntām mṛdulasvāntām kucabharatām tām namāmi śivakāntām.

राग : देश Rāga : Desh

6. अवटुतटघटित चूलीताडित तालीपलाशताटङ्कीं
वीणावादन वेलाकाम्पितशिरसं नमामि मातङ्गीं॥

avaṭutaṭaghaṭita cūlītāḍita tālīpalāśatāṭangīm
vīṇāvādana velākāmpitaśirasam namāmi mātangīm.

5. Sarigamapadhani

I prostrate before that Beloved of Siva, the Auspicious Lord, who is involved in the seven notes of Sa, Ri, Ga, Ma,
Pa, Dha, Ni,
the beauty of whose hands is reflected in the lute,
the gentle, soft natured one, bent by the burden of her breasts.

6. Avatutata

I bow to the daughter of Matanga
whose head shakes at the time of playing the lute,
and whose nape of the neck linked with hair is beaten by the green earrings.

राग : खमाज़ Rāga : Khamās

7. वीणारवानुषङ्गं विखच मुखाम्भोजमाधुरीभृङ्गं
करुणापूरतरङ्गं कलये मातङ्गकन्यकापाङ्गं ॥

vīṇāravānushankham vikhaca
mukhāmbhojamādhurībhṛngam
karuṇāpūratarangam kalaye mātangakanyakāpāngam.

राग : रीतिगौळ Rāga : Rītigowḷa

8. मणिभङ्गमेचकाङ्गीं मातङ्गीं नौमि सिद्धमातङ्गीं
यौवनवनसारङ्गीं सङ्गीताम्भोरुहानुभवभृङ्गीं ॥

maṇibhangamecakāngīm mātangīm naumi
siddhamātangīm
yauvanavanasārangīm
sangītāmbhoruhānubhavabhṛngīm.

7. Vīṇāravanushankham

I think of the glance of the daughter of *Mātanga*
which is filled with waves of compassion,
and is like the bee to the sweet honey of the full-blown lotus which is her face
which is closely attentive to the sound of the lute.

8. Maṇibhanga mecakangim

I prostrate before the daughter of Matanga,
who is the bee enjoying the lotus flower of music,
whose limbs are dark-blue like the sapphire,
who is like the spotted deer in the forest of youthfulness!

राग : मध्यमावति Rāga : Madhyamāvati

9. मेचकमासेचनकं मित्थ्या दृष्टान्तमध्यभागं ते
मातस्वरूपमनिशं मंगलसंगीतसौरभं वन्दे ॥

mecakamāsecanakam mitthyā
dṛṣṭāntamadhyabhāgam te
mātasvarūpamaniśam mangalasangītasaurabham
vande.

9. Mecakamāsecanakam

I ceaselessly venerate your form, Mother
which has the sweetness of auspicious music,
is dark-hued and wet (with perspiration)
and has a middle part which is almost non-existent.

SONGS OF KULASEKHARA PERUMAL

Song	*Raga*
1. Eradarttadum	Hamsadhwani
2. Aanaada selvattarampayargal	Sindhubhairavi
3. Chediyaaya valvinaigal	Mohanam
4. Taruduyaram tadaayelun	Sankarabharanam
5. Valaalaruttucchudinum	Abhogi
6. Venkantin kaliradarttai	Kamboji
7. Karumalar kkoontaloruttitannai	Abheri
8. Muntai nanmuraiyanbudai	Sri
9. Muzhudum vennaiyalaindu	Suruti
10. Vevvaayenvevvuraikettirunilattai	Madhyamavati

KULASEKHARA PERUMAL

KULASEKHARA PERUMAL (6th-7th Century A.D.)

Kulasekhara Perumal is one of the twelve *Ālwars,* the Vaishnavite religious poets of Tamil Nadu.

The *Ālwars* are so called because they are deemed to be "*immersed*" in the love of God.

The Alwars came from different backgrounds and social strata: There were Brahmins, Kshatriyas, non-Brahmins, cultivators and Harijans among them, but the intoxicating love of God unified them.

Kulasekhara was a King in Kerala. Though he was a competent ruler, he became preoccupied with spirituality and sacred lore.

The intensity of Kulasekhara's devotion is reflected in his songs.

In some of his songs, he has expressed a desire to be a stone in the Tirupati temple of Lord Venkateswara.

His involvement in the myths and legends of Lord Krishna and Lord Rama has produced some exquisite devotional poetry.

In one song, he identifies himself with *Devaki,* the biological mother of Krishna, from whom Krishna was taken away to Gokula where Nanda and Yasoda, the foster parents looked after him.

Kulasekhara expresses Devaki's desolation at being separated from her child and yearning for union with him again.

This is the same sense of sorrow of separation and yearning for union that pervades the outpourings of all the mystic poets of India.

राग : हंसध्वनि Rāga : Hamsadhwani

1. एऱडर्त्ततुं एनमाय्निलं
कीण्डतुं मुन्नि रामनाय्
माऱडर्त्ततुं मण्णळन्ततुं
चोल्लिप्पाडि् वण् पोन्निप्पे-
राऱुपोल्वरुं कण्णनीर्कोण्ड
रङ्कन् कोयिल् तिरुमुट्ट्रं,
चेऱुचेय्तोण्डर् चेवडिच्चेऴुञ्
चेऱेन्चेन्निक्कणिवने।

eṛaḍarttatum enamāynilam
keeṇḍatummunni rāmanāy,
māṛaḍarttatum maṇṇaḷantatum
collippaaḍi vaṇ ponnippe-
rārupolvarum kaṇṇaneerkoṇḍa
rankan koil tirumuṭṭram,
ceruceytoṇḍar cevaḍiccezhun
cerencennikkaṇivane.

1. Eradarttadum enamaynilam

I wish to wear on my head the dust of the feet
of those devotees of yours who have washed the frontyard
of your temple in Sri Rangam,
with their tears which welled up like the Kaveri river,
on singing of your glory and the greatness of your
incarnations for destroying the demons,
first as the boar (*Varaha*) lifting up the earth,
then as *Rama* destroying the lineage of demons,
and then as *Vāmana*, the dwarf, measuring the three
worlds with your feet.

राग : सिन्धु भैरवि Rāga : Sindhu Bhairavi

2. आनात चेल्व त्तरम्पैयर्कळ् तऱ्कुऴ़,
वानाळुं चेल्वमुं मण्णरशुं यान् वेण्डेन्
तेनार्पूञ्चोलैत्तिरुवेङ्कटच्चुनैयिल्
मीनाय् पिऱक्कुं वितियुडैयेनावेने।

aanaata celvattarampairkaḷ tarkuzha,
vaanaaḷum celvamum maṇṇaraśum yaan veṇḍen
tenaarpooncolaittiruvenkaṭaccunaiyil,
meenaay pirakkum vitiyuḍaiyenaavene.

2. Ānāda selvatarampayarkal

I do not want limitless wealth,
I do not want beautiful celestial women like *Rambha*,
I do not want the status of *Indra*, the Lord of celestials,
I do not want to be the overlord of this earth,
I desire to be born as a fish in the pond
in the Tirupati hills, full of gardens with flowers oozing honey.

राग : मोहनं

Rāga : Mohanam

3. चेडियाय वल्विनैकळ्
तीर्क्कुं तिरुमाले,
नेडियाने! वेङ्कटवा!
निन्कोयिलिन्वाशल्
अटियारुं वानवरु
मरम्पैयरुं किडन्तियङ्कुं,
पटियाय् क्किटन्तुन्
पवळवाय् काण्पेने॥

ceḍiyaaya valvinaikaḷ
teerkkum tirumaale,
neḍiyaane! venkaṭavaa!
nin koilin vaaśal,
aṭiyaarum vaanavaru
marampaiyarum kiḍantiyankum,
paṭiyāy kkiṭantun
pavaḷavaay kaaṇpene.

3. Chediyaya valvinaikal

O Lord who remove all the clusters of sin and evil that envelop me!
O Lord *Venkateswara*! Who stand tall in stature!
Let me be the doorstep in front of your temple,
on which pass your devotees, the celestials and angelic women!
So that I can see your coral-red lips!

राग : शंकराभरणं Rāga : Śankarābharaṇam

4. तरुतुयरं तडायेलुन्
चरणल्लाल् चरणिल्लै।
विरै़कुऴुवु मलर् प्पोऴि़ल्चूऴ्
विट्रुव क्कोट्टम्माने।
अरिचिनत्तालीन्ऱताय्
अकट्रिटिनुं मट्रवळ्तन्
अरुळ्निनैन्ते यऴुंकुऴ़वि
अतुवेपोन्ऱि़रुन्तेने।

tarutuyaram taḍāyelun
charaṇallāl charaṇillai
viraikuzhuvu malarppozhilchoozh
viṭṭruvakkoṭṭammaane
arichinattaaleenratāy
akaṭṭriṭinum maṭṭravaḷtan
aruḷninainte yazhumkuzhavi
atuveponriruntene.

4. Taruduyaram tadayelun

However much suffering you make me undergo

there is no refuge for me other than your feet!

O Lord! who reside in the holy place of *Vittuvakkotu*

surrounded by gardens of flowers exuding fragrance!

Even though the mother, in a fit of anger, pushes away the child!

It still cries for her cuddling affection!

Likewise am I!

राग : आभोगि Rāga : Ābhogi

5. वाळालरुत्तुच्चुडिनुं मरुत्तुवन्पाल्
माळातकातल्नोयाळन्पोल्, मायत्ताल्
मीळात्तुयर्तरिनुं विट्टुवक्कोट्टम्मा, नी
आळा वुनतरुळे पार्प्पनडियेने।

vaaḷaalaruttuccuḍinum maruttuvanpaal
maaḷaata kaatalnoyaaḷanpol, maayattaal
meeḷaattuyar tarinum viṭṭruvakkoṭṭammaa, nee
aaḷaa vunataruḷe paarppanaḍiyene.

5. Valalaruttucchudinum

Even though the doctor uses the surgical knife (to heal a wound),
The patient loves him (for he cures),
Likewise, even though you give me suffering hard to bear, by your mysterious ways,
I shall seek only your grace!
O Lord who dwell in *Vittuvakkotu*!

राग : कांबोजि Rāga : Kāmboji

6. वेङ्कण्तिण् कळिऱ्डर्त्ताय्
विट्रुवक्को ट्टम्माने,
एङ्कुप्पोयुय्केनुन्
निणैयडिये यडैयलल्लाल्,
एङ्कुं पोय् क्करैकाणा
तेरिकटल्वाय् मीण्डेयुं
वङ्कत्तिन् कूम्पेरुं
माप्परवै पोन्ऱेने।

venkaṇtiṇ kaḷiraḍarttaay
viṭṭruvakkoṭṭammaane,
enkuppoyuykenun
niṇaiyaḍiye yadaiyalallaal
enkum poy kkaraikaaṇaa
terikaṭalvaay meeṇḍeyum
vankattin koomperum
maapparavai ponrene.

6. Venkantin kaliradarttai

O Lord who dwell in *Vittuvakkotu*!
You are victorious over the mighty ones!
Other than seeking refuge at your feet, where else can I go?
Like the bird, which flies far and wide in search of land in mid ocean and returns to the flag mast of the ship,
So do I seek you, wandering helpless in the ocean of *Samsāra.**

---

*Phenomenal world.

राग : आभेरि Rāga : Ābheri

7. करुमलर्क्कून्तलोरुत्तितन्नैक्
कटैक्कणित्तु, आङ्के योरुत्तितन्पाल्
मरुवि मनंवैत्तु मट्ट्रोरुत्तिक्
कुऱैत्तौरु पेतैक्कुप्पोय्कुरित्तु
पुरिकुऴ्ल् मङ्कैयोरुत्तितन्नैप्
पुणर्त्ति यवळुक्कुं मेय्यनल्लै,
मरुतिरुत्ताय्! उन् वळर्त्तियूडे
वळर्किन्ऱ तालुन्ऱन् मायैताने।

karumalarkkoontaloruttitannaik
kaṭaikkaṇittu, aanke yoruttitanpaal
maruvi manamvaittu maṭṭṛoruttik
kuṛaittoru petaikkuppoykurittu,
purikuzhal mankaiyorutti tannaip
puṇartti yavaḷukkum maeyyanallai,
marutiruttaay! un vaḷarttiyooḍe
vaḷarkinra taalunran mayaitaane.

7. Karumalar kunta

You glance at a girl with dark hair adorned by flowers!

You act as if you have lost your heart to another girl!

You speak falsehood to yet another girl and dupe her!

At least you unite with another girl. Will you be true to her? No.

O Lord Krishna! who became the *Maruda* tree to destroy

demons

As you grow, your *Māyā*, magic and mystery grow!

राग : श्री Rāga : Śrī

8. मुन्तै नन्मुऱै यन्पुटैमकळीऱ्
मुऱैमुऱै तन्तं कुऱङ्किटैयिरुत्ति
एन्तैये! एन्ऱन् कुलप्पेरुञ्चुटरे!
एऴुमुकिल्कणत्तेऴिल्कवरेऱे
उन्तै यावन्? एन्ऱुरैप्पनिन्चेङ्केऴ्
विरलिनुं कटैक्कण्णिनुं काट्ट,
नन्दन् पेट्रनन् नल्विनैयिल्ला
नङ्कळ् कोन् वसुदेवन् पेट्रिलने।

muntai nanmurai yanpuṭaimakaḷeer
muraimurai tantam kurankiṭaiyirutti,
entaiye! enran kulapperuncuṭare!
ezhumukilkaṇattezhilkavarere
untai yaavan? enruraippanin cenkezh
viralinum kaṭaikkaṇṇinum kaaṭṭa,
nandan peṭṭranan nalvinai yillaa
nankaḷ kon vasudevan peṭṭrilane!

8. Muntai nanmurai

(Devaki, the real mother of Krishna laments)

The loving girls of Gokula
carry, by turns, child Krishna on their hips and ask him:
"Darling! who have lit up our lineage of Gokula,
O cloud-hued Krishna! Who is your father?"
And Krishna, by his rosy fingers and glance of the eye,
points to Nanda Gopa!
The good fortune of Nanda Gopa
my husband, Vasudeva does not have!

राग : सुरुटि Rāga : Suruṭi

9. मुऴ़ुतुं वेण्णैयळैन्तुतोट्टुण्णुं
मुकिऴ़िळञ्चिरु त्तामरैक्कैयुं,
एऴ़िल्कोळ् ताम्पुकोण्डडिप्पतर्केळ्कुं
निलयुं वेण्तयिर् तोय्न्त चेव्वायुं,
अऴ़ुकै युमञ्चि नोक्कुमन्नोक्कुं
अणिकोळ् चेञ्चिरु वाय् नेळिप्पतुवुं,
तोऴ़ुकै युमिवै कण्ड यशोदै
तोल्लै यिन्पत्तिरुति कण्डाळे।

muzhutum veṇṇaiyaḷaintutottuṇṇum
mukizhiḷanciru ttaamaraikkaiyum,
ezhilkoḷ taampukoṇḍaḍippatarkeḷkum
nilayum veṇtayir toynta cevvaayum,
azhukaiyumanci nokkumannokkum
aṇilkoḷ cenciru vaayneḷippatuvum,
tozhukaiyumivai kaṇḍa yaśodai
tollai yinpattiruti kaṇḍaaḷe.

9. Muzhutum vennai

(The scene described is that in which child Krishna, the butter thief, is caught red-handed by Yasoda)

The tender lotus hands are smeared all over with butter!

Yasoda pretends to beat him with the rope
Krishna stands with his reddish mouth dripping with curds and butter
and stares fearfully with tears in his eyes,
his beautiful mouth curling to cry,
and bowing as if he will never again steal butter!

Seeing this sight, Yasoda attained limitless bliss!

राग : मध्यमावति Rāga : Madhyamāvati

10. वेव्वायेन् वेव्वुरैके ट्टिरुनिलत्तै
वेण्डाते विरैन्तु, वेन्ऱ्
मैवायकळिऱोऴ़िन्तु तेरोऴ़िन्तु
मावोऴ़िन्तु वनमे मेवि,
नेय्वाय वेल्नेडुङ्कण् नेरिऴ़ैयुं
इळङ्कोवुं पिन्पु पोक,
एव्वाऱ् नटन्तनै यें इरामावो
एं पेरुमान्! एन् चेय्केने।

vevvaayen vevvurai keṭṭirunilattai
veṇḍaate viraintu, venri
maivaayakaḷirozhintu terozhintu
maavozhintu vaname mevi,
neyvaaya velneḍunkaṇ nerizhaiyum
iḷankovum pinpu poka,
evvaaru naṭantanai yem iraamaavo
em perumaan! en ceykene.

10. Vevvayen vevvurai

O Lord Rama!
Listening to Kaikeyi's words and to protect your father's promise,
giving up the crown, the land, wealth, elephants, chariots, horses, army, etc.,
accompanied by the bow-eyed Sita and brother Lakshmana,
How did you walk to the forest, your legs paining?
My Lord! I cannot bear this!

SONGS OF KAMBAN

Song	*Raga*
1. Vaanin nizhintu	Bhoopalam
2. Vedangal araikinra	Atana
3. Oyaada malarayane	Mohanam
4. Nee aadi paramparamum	Bhairavi
5. Taay tannai ariyaada	Sahana
6. Aravaakicchumattiyaal	Suddhasaveri
7. Annamaay arumaraigal	Ritigowla
8. Moolame illaada mutalvane	Hindolam
9. Nirkum neduneetta neeril	Sindhubhairavi
10. Moolamum natuvum eerum	Madhyamavati

KAMBAN

KAMBAN (9th Century A.D.)

Kamban, the Tamil poet who was the first to write the epic *Ramayana* in a regional language, is the pride of Tamil Nadu and Tamil language.

Subramania Bharati eulogises Kamban by saying "Tamilnadu is the state where Kamban was born".

Kamban's deep devotion to God, incarnate as Lord Rama, pervades every stanza in *Kamba Ramayana*, a work comprising 11000 stanzas.

It is claimed that the devotional lyrics of the *Alwars* had a profound influence on Kamban.

Biographical details about Kamban are scanty. He is believed to have been born the son of a weaver named Adityan.

Tiruvazhundur in Tanjavur district of Tamil Nadu has been mentioned as the birthplace of Kamban.

The name *Kamban* is unique, presumably it is derived from the Tamil word for a pillar, near which he was discovered by the Chola King.

Kamban is called *Kavi Chakravarti*, "the Emperor among poets". Kamban's poetry, rich in lyrical quality, and conceptual grandeur, has been compared to that of Keats, Swinburne and Milton.

He is the Tamil equivalent of the Hindi poet Tulsidas.

The literary embellishments in Kamban's songs achieve greatness, because of his deep devotion to God, whom he saw as Rama, the Supreme Saviour.

राग : भूपालं Rāga : Bhoopālam

1. वानिन् निऴ़िन्तु वरं पिकन्त
माऴ़तन्तिन् वेप्पेङ्कुं
ऊनुं उयिरुं उणर्वुंपोल् उळ्ळुं
पुऱन्तुं ऊनेन्प-
कूनुं चिऱिय कोत्तायुं
कोटुमै इऴ़ैप्प कोल् तुऱन्तु
कानुं कटलुं कटन्तु इमैयोर्
इटुक्कण् तीर्त्त कऴ़ल् वेन्तन्।

vaanin nizhintu varampikanta
maazhatantin veppenkum

oonum uyirum uṇarvumpol uḷḷum

purantum ūnenpa-

koonum ciriya kottaayum

koṭumai izhaippa kol tuṛantu

kaanum kaṭalum kaṭantu imaiyor

iṭukkaṇ teertta kazhal ventan.

1. Vānin nizhintu

Subject to the cruelty of the hunchback (*Mandhara*)
and stepmother (*Kaikeyi*),
Losing the royal sceptre, he crossed the forest and ocean and killing demons like Ravana,
removed the distress of the celestials,
King Rama, who wore the victorious anklet,
Is the incarnation of God, the body and soul, residing
inside and outside of the world comprising
the earth, water, fire, wind and the sky.

राग : अटाना Rāga : Aṭānā

2. वेदङ्कळ् अऱैकिन्ऱ् उलकेङ्कुं विरिन्तनवुन्
पादङ्कळ् इवैयेन्निन् पटिवङ्कळ् एप्पटियो?
ओदङ्कोळ् कटलन्ऱि ओन्ऱिनोडु ओन्ऱोव्वाप्-
पूतङ्कळ् तोऱुं उऱैन्ताल् अवै उन्नै पोऱुक्कुमो?

vedankaḷ araikinra ulakenkum virintanavun
paadankaḷ ivaiyennin paṭivankaḷ eppaṭiyo?
odankoḷ kaṭalanri onrinoḍu onrovvaap-
pootankaḷ torum uraintaal avai unnai porukkumo?

2. Vedangal araikinra

Your feet, praised by the Vedas, are spread all over the world.
If your feet are thus, what to say of your holy form?
If, instead of residing in the cold ocean,
you decide to dwell in other elements or objects,
can they bear you? (Definitely not.)

(Only the ocean can bear your form.)

राग : मोहनं Rāga : Mohanam

3. ओयात मलरयने मुतलाक उळराकि
मायात वानवर्क्कुं मट्ट्रोऴिन्त मन्नुयिर्क्कुं
नी आदि मुतल्तातै नेरिमुरैयाल् ईन्ऱेट्टुत्त
तायावार यावरे? तरुमत्तिन् तनिमूर्त्ति।

oyaata malarayane mutalaaka uḷaraaki
maayaata vaanavarkkum maṭṭrozhinta mannuyirkkum
nee aadi mutal taatai nerimuraiyaal īnreṭutta
taayaavaara yaavare? tarumattin tanimūrtti.

3. Oyāda malarayane

O Embodiment of righteousness!

You are the Primordial father of Brahma, the Creator

who is ceaselessly engaged in the act of creation,

residing in the lotus,

as also of other immortal celestials and other living beings.

If so, who is their rightful mother?

राग : भैरवि

Rāga : Bhairavi

4. नी आदि परंपरमुं निन्नवे उलकङ्कळ्
आयात चमयमुं निन् अटियवे अयल् इल्लै
तीयारिन् ओळित्तियाल् वेळिनिन्ऱाल् तीङ्कु उण्डो?
वीयात पेरुमाय विळैयाट्टुं वेण्टुमो?

nee aadi paramparamum ninnave ulakankaḷ
aayaata camayamum nin aṭiyave ayal illai
teeyaarin oḷittiyaal veḷininraal teenku uṇḍo?
veeyaata perumaaya viḷaiyaaṭṭum veṇṭumo?

4. Ni adi paramparamum

You are the primordial Supreme Being!
All the worlds are yours!
All the Vedas worthy of being understood are subordinate to you!
Why do you remain hidden, like evildoers?
Why don't you disclose yourself (as the Supreme Being)?
If it is known who you are, what harm will result?
Is this magical, mystical sport necessary?

राग : सहाना Rāga : Sahānā

5. ताय् तन्नै अऱियात कन्ऱिल्लै; तन् कन्ऱै
आयुं अऱियुं; उलकिन् तायाकिन् ऐय!
नी अऱिति एप्पोरुळ्ुं अवै उन्नै निलै अऱिया
मायै इतु एन् कोलो? वाराते वरवल्लाय्?

taay tannai ariyaata kanrillai; tan kanrai
aayum ariyum; ulakin taayaakin ayya!
nee ariti epporuḷum avai unnai nilai ariyaa
maayai itu en kolo? vaaraate varavallāy?

5. Tai tannai ariyada

There is no calf which cannot recognize its mother cow.
The mother cow will also identify its calf.
O Lord, who are the Mother of the universe!
You know all things!
What is this *Maya* (illusion) that the worldly beings do not recognize you?
Why don't they understand that you are the incarnation of God?

राग : शुद्धसावेरि Rāga : Śuddhasāveri

6. अऱवाकिच्चुमत्तियाल् अयिल् एयिट्ट्रिन् एन्तुतियाल्
ओरुवायिन् विऴुङ्कुतियाल् ओरटियाल् ओळित्तियाल्
तिरुवान निलमकळै ईतरिन्ताल् चीऱाळो
मरुवारुं तुऴायलङ्कल् मणिमार्पिन् वैकुवाळ्?

aṛavaakiccumattiyaal ayil eyiṭṭrin entutiyaal
oruvaayin vizhunkutiyaal oraṭiyaal oḷittiyaal
tiruvaana nilamakaḷai eetarintaal ceeraaḷo
maruvaarum tuzhāyalankal maṇimaarpin vaikuvaaḷ?

6. Aravaki chumattiyal

You bear this earth in the form of Adi Sesha, the Serpent
Chief!
As the incarnation of *Varaha*, the Boar, you lift up the
earth with your sharp horns!
At the time of deluge you swallow the earth in one gulp!
In the incarnation of *Vāmana*, the Dwarf, you measured
the earth in one step!
Doesn't *Bhu Devi** who resides on your chest get
angry with all these deeds?

*Mother Earth.

राग : रीतिगौळ Rāga : Rītigowḷa

7. अन्नमाय् अरुमऱ़ैकळ् अऱ़ैन्ताय् नी अवै उन्नै
मुन्नमाऱ़् ओतुवित्तार्? एल्लारुं मुटिन्तारो?
पिन्नमाय् ओन्ऱाताल् पिरिन्तेयो? पिरियातो?
एन्न मामायं इवै? एनमाय् मण् इटन्ताय्?

annamaay arumaṛaikaḷ aṛaintaay nee avai unnai
munnamaar otuvittaar? ellārum muṭintaaro?
pinnamaay onrātaal pirinteyo? piriyaato?
enna maamaayam ivai? enamaay maṇ iṭantaay?

7. Annamai arumaraigal

In the form of the swan, you taught the Vedas to
Brahma, the creator!
Before that who taught you the Vedas?
Have they disappeared?
You are the Supreme Being,
Who remain separated from and united with everything in the world!
What is this mysterious magic?

राग : हिन्दोलं Rāga : Hindolam

8. मूलमे इल्ला मुतल्वने! नी मुयलुं
कोलमो यार्क्कुं तेरिवऱिय कोळ्कैयवाल्
आलमो? आलिन् अटैयो? अटैक्किटन्त
बालनो? वेलैपरप्पो? पकराये?

moolame illaa mutalvane! nee muyalum
kolamo yaarkkum terivariya koḷ kaiyavaal
aalamo? aalin aṭaiyo? aṭaikkiṭanta
bālano? velaiparappo? pakaraaye!

8. Mūlame illada

You are the sourceless, Primordial One!
No one fully understands the forms you manifest in!
Are you the Banyan tree which appears at the time of deluge?
Are you the leaf of that Banyan tree?
Are you the infant lying on that Banyan leaf?
Or are you the vast ocean?
(What is your true form?)

राग : सिन्धु भैरवि Rāga : Sindhu Bhairavi

9. निर्कुं नेटु नीत्त नीरिल् मुळैत्तेऴुन्त
मोक्कुळे पोल मुऱण् इट्ट्र अण्डङ्कळ्
ओक्क उयर्न्तु उन्नुळे तोन्ऱि ओळिक्किन्ऱ
पक्कं अऱितर्कु एळितो? परंपरने!

nirkum neṭu neetta neeril muḷaittezhunta
mokkuḷe pola muraṇ iṭṭra aṇḍankaḷ
okka uyarntu unnuḷe tonri oḷikkinra
pakkam aṛitarku eḷito? paramparane!

9. Nirkum nedu nitta

In the flood which appears at the time of deluge,
the small eggs which appear as droplets of water grow
big and then again get dissolved in you!
O Supreme One!
Is it easy to understand this phenomenon?

राग : मध्यमावति Rāga : Madhyamāvati

10. मूलमुं नटुवुं ईनुं इल्लतोर् मुममैत्ताय्
कालमुं कणक्कुं नीत्त कारणन् कैविल् एन्ति
चूलमुं तिकिरि चङ्कुं करकमुं तुऱन्तु तोल्लै
आलमुं मलरुं वेळ्ळिप्पोरुप्पुं विट्टु अयोत्ति वन्तान्।

moolamum naṭuvum eenum illator mumamaittaay
kaalamum kaṇakkum neetta kāraṇan kaivil enti
coolamum tikiri cankum karakamum turantu tollai
aalamum malarum veḻḻipporuppum viṭṭu ayotti vantaan.

10. Mulamum natuvum

That Supreme Being who has no beginning, middle or end and transcends the three periods of time: past, present and future,

gave up the trident, the conch, discus and the water bowl and the residence in the banyan leaf, the lotus and the Kailasa mountain

appeared in Ayodhya as Rama, holding the bow in his hand!

(The poet conceives of Rama as the incarnation of the Trinity Brahma, Vishnu and Siva.)

SONGS OF DEVARA DASIMAYYA

Song	*Raga*
1. Saagaradolagana kinchina	Bagesri
2. Urivakendadamele	Begada
3. Arthavuntendahamkarisi	Desh
4. Aaseparinaamakke	Yamuna Kalyana
5. Nee neesaneeyade	Hamsanandi
6. Oretegala kandintu	Mohanam
7. Edaradasidalli mrida nimma	Nadanamakriya
8. Hara tanna bhaktara	Khamas
9. Nishteyulla bhakta	Tilang
10. Anubhaavanilladavana	Madhyamavati

DEVARA DASIMAYYA

DEVARA DASIMAYYA (10th Century A.D.)

Devara Dasimayya is the pioneer propagator of the *Veera Saivite* spiritual tradition, whose later luminaries include such stalwarts as Basavanna, Mahadevi Akka and Allama Prabhu.

Veera Saivism was a movement devoted to the worship of God as Siva and rejected social inequalities.

Devara Dasimayya was born in the village of *Mudanduru* in Karnataka in the tenth century A.D.

The village had a temple dedicated to Siva, as *Rāmanātha*, Siva as worshipped by Rama.

All songs of Devara Dasimayya are addressed to Ramanatha.

Convinced that working in the world was part of worship of the Lord and a means to realise Him, Dasimayya became a weaver. He married *Duggale*, who was a devoted wife to him.

Dasimayya was a vigorous proponent of Saivism.

The King in whose kingdom he lived was a Chalukyan ruler, named Jayasimha, who was a follower of Jainism.

Legend has it that Devara Dasimayya converted the King to Saivism through a series of miracles.

As a result of his passionate espousal of Saivism, people of all beliefs: jungle tribes and Brahmins, became his followers.

He laid emphasis on faith, devotion and surrender to God.

There is a story that when he wanted to give up the world, Dasimayya went to his native village, Mudanduru and told the Deity in the temple, Ramanatha: "I've lived my life and now you must return me to yourself."

The Lord obliged and both Dasimayya and his wife joined the infinite.

राग : बागेश्री Rāga : Bāgeśrī

1. सागरदोळगण किञ्चिन साकारदन्ते
ससियोळगण फलपुष्पङ्गळ परिमळदन्ते
मनद मरेयमातु नेनेहिनल्लरिदु
नालगे नोडिवागलल्लदे
काणबारदु केळबारदु
ओन्दङ्गदोळडगिद नूरोन्दरपरि
रामनाथा!

saagaradoḷagaṇa kincina saakaaradante
sasiyoḷagaṇa phalapushpangaḷa parimaḷadante
manada mareyamaatu nenehinallaridu
naalage noḍivaagalallade
kaaṇabaaradu keḷabaaradu
ondangadoḷaḍagida noorondarapari
rāmanāthā!

1. Sagaradolagana

You are
like the minute particle hidden in the womb of the ocean,
like the fragrance of flowers hidden in the sapling,
(you are) like the deepest emotion brought to memory
and spoken by the tongue,
We cannot see you or hear you!
You are the meaning of a hundred words hidden inside one word!

O Ramanatha! O Lord of Rama!

राग : बेगडा Rāga : Begaḍā

2. उरिवकेण्डदमेले तृणवतन्दिरिसिदरे
आतृणव केण्डनुङ्गिदन्ते-
गुरुचरणदमेले तनु तृणवनिळुहिदरे
आतनसर्वाङ्गवेल्ला लिङ्गकाणा
रामनाथा!

urivakeṇḍadamele tṛṇavataṇdirisidare
aatṛṇava keṇḍanungidante-
gurucaraṇadamele tanu tṛṇavaniḷuhidare
aatanasarvaangavellaa lingakaaṇaa
rāmanāthā!

2. Urivakendadamele

If a blade of grass is placed on a burning ember,
that blade of grass is consumed by the ember!
Likewise, if the body is surrendered at the Master's feet,
that body in all its limbs becomes one with the Lord!
O Ramanatha! O Lord of Rama!

राग : देश Rāga : Desh

3. अर्थवुण्टेन्दहङ्करिसि
माडुवन भक्ति तोत्तिन (कूटदत्तूरिय)
मेळदन्ते
तनु-मन-धन-दल्लि वञ्चनयुळ्ळ
प्रपञ्चिय मनेयकूळु
शुनकनबाय एलुव प्रतिशुनक
तिन्दन्ते काणा रामनाथा!

arthavuṇṭendahankarisi
maaḍuvana bhakti tottina (kooṭadattūriya)
meḷadante
tanu-mana-dhana-dalli vancanayuḷḷa
prapanciya maneyakooḷu
śunakanabaaya eluva pratiśunaka
tindante kaaṇaa rāmanāthā!

3. Arthavuntendahamkarisi

The devotion of a person,
arrogant on account of his wealth,
is deception in body, mind and wealth.
Food served in such a person's home
is like food snatched by one dog from another dog's mouth!
O Ramanatha! O Lord of Rama!

राग : यमुना कल्याण Rāga : Yamunā Kalyāṇa

4. आसेपरिणामक्के बेसत्तु होयित्तु
आश्रयद निद्रे केट्टित्तु ग्रासमेल्लनायित्तु
स्त्रीयरिच्छे केट्टित्तु
ईश्वर, निम्म पादाम्बुजसेवयिन्द
रामनाथा!

aasepariṇaamakke besattu hoyittu
aaśrayada nidre keṭṭittu graasamellanaayittu
streeyaricche keṭṭittu
īśvara, nimma pādāmbujasevayinda
rāmanāthā!

4. Āseparinamakke

Greed results in a frustrated mind!
But serving your lotus feet, O Lord!,
gives restful sleep,
satisfaction of the palette,
desire for woman fulfilled!
O Ramanatha! O Lord of Rama!

राग : हंसानन्दि Rāga : Hamsānandi

5. नी नीसनीयदे मानिस नीवने?
नी नीसुवकारण मानिसनीवनु
मानिसन हृदयदोळहोक्कु
नी नार्सुव कारण
नी ने शरणेम्बनय्या,
रामनाथा!

nee neesaneeyade maanisa neevane?
nee neesuvakaaraṇa maanisaneevanu
maanisana hṛdayadoḷahokku
nee naarsuva kaaraṇa
nee ne śaraṇembanayyaa,
rāmanāthā!

5. Ni nisaniyade

If you do not give, can man give?
Because you give, man gives!
You are in the heart of man!
Since it is you who give,
I seek refuge in you!
O Ramanatha! O Lord of Rama!

राग : मोहनं Rāga : Mohanam

6. ओरेतेगळ कण्डिन्तु केलरु भावियतोडेम्बरु
अरवट्टिगे उत्रवु तम्मदेम्बरु
सुरिव मळे सुरियदिर्दडे
अवरेतरल्लि नीडुवरय्या रामनाथा?
इळे निम्म दाना बेळे निम्म दाना
सुळिदु सूसुव वायु निम्म दाना
निम्म दानवनुण्डु अन्यरहोळगवा
कुन्निगळने नेम्बे हेळा रामनाथा!

oretegaḷa kaṇḍintu kelaru bhaaviyatoḍembaru
aravaṭṭige utravu tammadembaru
suriva maḷe suriyadirdaḍe
avaretaralli neeḍuvarayyaa rāmanāthā?
iḷe nimma daanaa beḷe nimma daanaa
suḷidu sūsuva vaayu nimma daanaa
nimma daanavanuṇḍu anyarahoḷagavaa
kunnigaḷane nembe heḷaa rāmanāthā!

6. Oretegaḷa kandintu

Seeing the sudden sprout of water, some people attribute

it to their devotion!

Wealth contained in a half empty box they think is theirs!

If the cloud, laden with raindrops, does not rain,

with what will they give, O Ramanatha! Lord of Rama!

This earth is your gift!

Plants and flowers are your gift!

The bounteous wind is your gift!

Having enjoyed your gifts, they praise others!

What do you say of such low beings!

O Ramanatha! O Lord of Rama!

राग : नादनामक्रिया Rāga : Nādanāmakriyā

7. एडरडसिदल्लि मृड निम्म नेनवरु
एडरडसिद विपत्तु कडेयागलोडने
मृड निम्म नेडहियू काणरु रामनाथा!

eḍaraḍasidalli mṛḍa nimma nenavaru
eḍaraḍasida vipattu kaḍeyaagaloḍane
mṛḍa nimma neḍahiyū kaaṇaru rāmanāthā!

7. Edaradasidalli

O Lord!
When difficulties arise, people think of you!
When they get over the difficulties, they will not,
even by chance, trip on a thought of you!
O Lord! O Ramanatha! Lord of Rama!

राग : खमाज़ Rāga : Khamās

8. हर तन्न भक्तर तिरिवन्ते माडुव
ओरेदु नोडुव सुवर्णद चिन्नदन्ते
अरेदु नोडुव चन्दनदन्ते
अरिदु नोडुव कम्बिन कोलिनन्ते
बेदरदे बेच्चदे इद्दडे
करविडि देत्तिकोम्ब नम्म रामनाथनु!

hara tanna bhaktara tirivante maaḍuva
oredu noḍuva suvarṇada cinnadante
aredu noḍuva candanadante
aridu noḍuva kambina kolinante
bedarade beccade iddaḍe
karaviḍi dettikomba namma rāmanāthanu!

8. Hara tanna bhaktara

God, the Almighty tests His devotees
As gold is tested by rubbing on the whetstone, He rubs us.
As sandal paste is extracted from sandalwood by grinding,
He grinds us.
He chews us as the sugarcane is chewed (to extract juice)
If the devotee does not get frightened nor is shaken,
He stretches His arms and lifts,
Our Ramanatha, Lord of Rama!

राग : तिलंग Rāga : Tilang

9. निष्ठेयुळ्ळ भक्त नट्टडवियलिद्दडेनु
अदु पट्टणवेन्देनिसुवुदु
निष्ठेयिल्लद भक्त पट्टपादल्लिद्दडू
नट्टडविकाणा रामनाथा ॥

nishṭheyuḷḷa bhakta naṭṭaḍaviyaliddaḍenu
adu paṭṭaṇavendenisuvudu
nishṭheyillada bhakta paṭṭapaadalliddaḍū
naṭṭaḍavikaaṇaa rāmanāthā!

9. Nishteyulla bhakta

The faithful devotee,
even if he is in deep forest,
feels as if he is in town,
The devotee, devoid of faith,
even if he is in a town,
feels as if he is in a forest!
O Ramanatha! O Lord of Rama!

राग : मध्यमावति Rāga : Madhyamāvati

10. अनुभावविल्लदवन भक्ति
तलेक्केळगादुदय्या
अनुभाव भक्तिगाधार
अनुभाव भक्तिगे नेलेवने
अनुभाववुळ्ळवर कण्डु तुर्य
संभाषणेय बेसगोळ्ळदिद्दरे
नरकदल्लिक्कय्या रामनाथा!

anubhāvavilladavana bhakti
talekkeḷagaadudayyaa
anubhāva bhaktigaadhaara
anubhāva bhaktige nelevane
anubhāvavuḷḷavarakaṇḍu turya
sambhāshaṇeya besagoḷḷadiddare
narakadallikkayyaa rāmanāthā!

10. Anubhavavilladavana

The devotion of one, who has no faith,
is lower than earth.
Faith is the foundation of devotion.
Faith is the shelter for devotion.
If one does not meet the faithful
and pick up conversation,
it is like being in hell!
O Ramanatha! Lord of Rama!

SONGS OF GURU RAMDAS

	Song	*Raga*
1.	Ram ram raamai ant na paayiya	Kalyan
2.	Japi man ram naam pargaas	Kanada
3.	Ram ram boli boli khojte badbhaagee	Malhar
4.	Govind charanan kau balihaaree	Saranga
5.	Rama naamu ratan kothdee gadh mandari	Vasanta
6.	Hari ka santu hari ki hari moorati	Bhairav
7.	Hari hari bhagati bhare bhandara	Maru
8.	Gun gaava gun vithara gun boli	Sri
9.	Hari padu hari likhoo hari japi	Dhanasree
10.	Harigun gaave hau tisu balihaari	Devagandhari

GURU RAMDAS

GURU RAMDAS (1534 A.D.-1581 A.D.)

Guru Ramdas is the fourth Sikh Guru, among the ten Gurus of Sikhism.

The ten gurus are: *Guru Nanak,* the founder of Sikhism, *Guru Angad,* Nanak's disciple, *Guru Amardas,* Angad's disciple, *Guru Ramdas,* Amardas's son-in-law, *Guru Arjan Dev,* Ramdas's son, *Guru Hargobind,* Arjan Dev's son, *Guru Har Rai,* Hargobind's grandson, *Guru Hari Krishen,* Har Rai's son, *Guru Teg Bahadur,* Hargobind's son and *Guru Gobind Singh,* Teg Bahadur's son.

Credit goes to Guru Ramdas for having got a large tank dug, around which the city of Amritsar was built by his son Arjan Dev.

All the Sikh Gurus were profoundly influenced by the exponents of the Bhakti movement, and all their songs emphasize the chanting of the Lord's name as a means to liberation. Guru Ramdas is no exception.

The preaching of Guru Nanak pervades the songs of Guru Ramdas:

"There is One God. His entity is the Truth. He is the Creator. He is without fear. He is without enmity. Of timeless form, He never dies or takes birth. He is self-effulgent. He can be realised only through His grace."

This is not different from the Hindu concept of Godhead.

Another remarkable fact to be noted is that Guru Ramdas, like all the other Sikh Gurus, refers to God as *Hari, Ram, Govind, Madhusudan, Murari, Narahari,* etc. all of them Vaishnavite epithets applied to God.

राग : कल्याण Rāga : Kalyāṇa

1. रामा रम रामै अंतु न पाइआ॥
हम बारिक प्रतिपारे तुमरे तू बड पुरखु पिता मेरा माइआ॥
हरि के नाम असंख अगम हहि अगम अगम हरि राइआ॥
गुणी गिआनी सुरति बहु कीनी इकु तिलु नही कीमति पाइआ॥
गोबिंद गुण गोबिंद सद गावहि गुन गोबिंद अंतु न पाइआ॥
तू अमिति अतोलु अपरंपार सुआमी बहु जपीऔ थाह न पाइआ॥
उसतति करहि तुमरी जन माधौ गुन गावहि हरि राइआ॥
तुम्ह जल निधि हम मीने तुमरे तेरा अंतु न कतहू पाइआ॥
जन कउ किरपा करहु मधुसूदन हरि देवहु नामु जपाइआ॥
मैं मूरख अंधुले नामु टेक है जन नानक गुरमुखि पाइआ॥

rāmā rama raamai antu na paayiaa
ham baarik pratipaare tumre tū baḍa purakhu pitaa merā māyiaa
hari ke naam asankh agam hahi agam agam hari raayiaa
guṇee gyaanee surati bahu keenee iku tilu nahi keemati pāyiaa
gobind guṇ gobind sad gaavahi gun gobind antu na paayiaa
tū amiti atolu aparampār suaamī bahu japīai thaah na paayiaa
ustati karhi tumari jan maadhau gun gaavahi hari raayiaa
tumh jal nidhi ham meene tumre terā antu na katahu paayiaa
jan kau kripaa karhu madhusūdan hari devahu naamu japaaiaa
main moorakh andhule naamu ṭek hai jan nānak gurumukhi paaiaa.

1. Rama ram ramai

   Delight in reciting Rama's name is endless!
   We devotees deem you as our ancestral father and mother!
   Hari's names are countless!
   The Vedas are Hari's words!
   The good scientist remembers many things but does not attain anything valuable!
   Those who sing of the glory of Govind have no end!
   You are the limitless, immeasurable immortal Lord!
   There is no limit to the recounting of your qualities!
   When your devotees sing your praises, you, Hari, become manifest!
   You are the ocean and we are fish!
   There is no end for you!
   People say: O *Madhusudana*!* Show mercy and sing your praises!
   I, the blind idiot, depend on your name, through the mouth of my Guru Nanak!

---

*Killer of the demon Madhu.

राग : कानडा Rāga : Kānaḍā

2. जपि मन राम नाम परगास ॥
हरि के संत मिलि प्रीति लगानी विचे गिरह उदास ॥
हम हरि हिरदै जपिओ नामु नरहरि प्रभि क्रिपा करी किरपास ॥
अनदिनु अनदु भइआ मनु बिगसिआ उदमु भए मिलन की आस ॥
हम हरि सुआमी प्रीति लगाई जितने सास लीए हम ग्रास ॥
किलबिख दहन भए खिन अंतरि तूटि गए माइआ के फास ॥
किआ हम किरम किआ करम कमावहि मूरख मुगध रखे प्रभ तास ॥
अवगनीआरे पाथर भारे सतसंगति मिलि तरे तरास ॥
जेती स्रिसटि करी जगदीसरि ते सभि ऊच हम नीच बिखिआस ॥
हमरे अवगुन संगि गुर मेटे जन नानक मेलि लीए प्रभ पास ॥

japi man rām nām pargaas
hari ke sant mili preeti lagaanee vice girah udās
ham hari hiradai japio nāmu narahari prabhi kripaa karī kirpaas
anadinu anadu bhaiaa manu bigsiaa udamu bhae milan kī aas
ham hari suaamee preeti lagaai jitne saas līye ham graas
kilbikh dahan bhae khin antari tuṭi gaye maaiaa ke phaas
kiaa ham kiram kiaa karam kamaavahi moorakh mugadh rakhe prabh taas
avaganīaare pāthar bhaare satsangati mili tare taraas
jeti srisaṭi karī jagadeesari te sabhi ūch ham neech bikhiaas
hamre avagun sangi gur meṭe jan nānak meli leeye prabh paas.

2. Japi man ram nam

O mind! recite the name of Rama!
We have met Hari's sages and are happy and left behind all sorrow!
We recite Hari's name in our minds,
O Lord! O Narahari! O compassionate One! Show mercy!
Every day, the mind gets filled with joy and eager effort in the hope of meeting the Lord!
We are happy in Lord Hari by whose breath we breathe!
All sins have got burnt, all fears dispelled inside the mind!
Who are we? What is our action?
We are dumb animals with whom the Lord plays!
By the company of good sages, we got relief from the burden of *samsāra*!
When we pray to the Lord of the universe, we get the knowledge that we are low and everything is high!
The teacher removes all our bad qualities,
Guru Nanak takes us near the Lord!

राग : मल्हार Rāga : Malhār

3. राम राम बोलि बोलि खोजते बडभागी ॥
हरि का पंथु कोऊ बतावै हउ ता कै पाइ लागी ॥
हरि हमारो मीतु सखाई हम हरि सिउ प्रीति लागी ॥
हरि हम गावहि हरि हम बोलहि अउरु दुतीआ प्रीति हम तिआगी ॥
मनमोहन मोरो प्रीतम रामु हरि परमानंदु बैरागी ॥
हरि देखे जीवत है नानकु इक निमख पलो मुखि लागी ॥

rām rām boli boli khojte baḍbhaagī
hari kā panthu koū bataave hau taa kai paai laagee
hari hamāro meetu sakhāi ham hari siu preeti laagī
hari ham gaavahi hari ham bolhi auru duteeaa preeti ham tiāgī
manmohan moro preetam rāmu hari paramānandu bairaagee
hari dekhe jeevat hai nānaku ik nimakh palo mukhi laagee.

3. Ram ram boli

The fortunate ones seek Ram, chanting Ram, Ram!
Will someone show the way to Hari?
so that we can reach Him!
Hari is our dear friend!
We love Hari!
We sing of Hari, we speak of Hari and we gladly give up this world!
Ram is my beloved charming my heart!
Hari is the blissful recluse!
Nanak has taught us that seeing Hari is real living!

राग : सारंग Rāga : Sāranga

4. गोबिंद चरनन कउ बलिहारी॥
भवजलु जगतु न जाई तरणा जपि हरि हरि पारि उतारी॥
हिरदै प्रतीति बनी प्रभ केरी सेवा सुरति बीचारी॥
अनदिनु राम नामु जपि हिरदै सरब कला गुणकारी॥
प्रभु अगम अगोचरु रविआ सरब ठाई मनि तनि अलख अपारी॥
गुर किरपाल भए तब पाइआ हिरदै अलखु लखारी॥
अंतरि हरि नामु सरब धरणीधर साकत कउ दूरि भइआ अहंकारी॥
त्रिसना जलत न कबहू बूझहि जूऐ बाजी हारी॥
ऊठत बैठत हरि गुन गावहि गुरि किंचत किरपा धारी॥
नानक जिन कउ नंदरि भई है तिन की पैज सवारी॥

gobind caranan kau balihārī
bhavajalu jagatu na jaaee taraṇaa japi hari hari pāri utārī
hiradai prateetī banī prabh kerī sevaa surati bīcaarī
anadinu rām nāmu japi hiradai sarab kalaa guṇkaaree
prabhu agam agocaru raviaa sarab ṭhaaī mani tani alakh apārī
gur kirapaal bhae tab paaiaa hiradai alakhu lakhārī
anatari hari naamu sarab dharaneedhar saakat kau doori bhaiaa ahamkārī
trisana jalat na kabhū boojhhi jūai baajee haarī
ūṭhat baiṭhat hari gun gaavahi guri kincat kirapaa dhaaree
nānak jin kau nadari bhaī hai tin kī paij savaaree.

4. Govind charanan

I am delighted in the feet of Govinda!

We can cross the ocean of *Samsara*, reciting the name of Hari!

The heart is pleased that it can serve the Lord and meditate on Him!

Reciting Ram's name every day makes the heart filled with all good qualities!

The Lord is the incomprehensible, imperceptible Sun who is beyond all minds and bodies, limitless!

Due to the kindness of the teacher, one has attained in the heart the unseeable Lord!

Once Hari's name is established in the heart, all fear and

arrogance are dispelled!

राग : वसंत Rāga : Vasanta

5. राम नामु रतन कोठड़ी गड़ मंदरि एक लुकानी ॥
सतिगुरु मिलै त खोजीअै मिलि जोती जोति समानी ॥
माधो साधू जन देहू मिलाई ॥
देखत दरसु पाप सभि नासहि पवित्र परम पदु पाई ॥
पंच चोर मिलि लागे नगरीआ राम नाम धनु हिरिआ ॥
गुरमति खोज परे तब पकरे धनु साबतु रासि उबरिआ ॥
पाखंड भरम उपाव करि थाके रिद अंतरि माइआ माइआ ॥
साधू पुरखु पुरखपति पाइआ अगिआन अंधेरु गवाइआ ॥
जगनाथ जगदीस गुसांई करि किरपा साधु मिलावै ॥
नानक सांति होवै मन अंतरि नित हिरदै हरि गुण गावै ॥

rām nāmu ratan koṭhaḍee gaḍ mandari ek lukānī
satiguru milai ta khojeeai mili jotee joti samānī
mādho sādhū jan dehū milaaī
dekhat darsu paap sabhi naasahi pavitr param padu paaī
panc cor mili lāge nagarīaa rām nām dhanu hiriaa
gurmati khoj pare tab pakare dhanu saabatu raasi ubariaa
paakhaṇḍ bharam upaav kari thaake rid antari maaiaa maaiaa
saadhū purakhu purakhpati paaiaa agiaan andheru gavaaiaa
jaganaath jagadees gusaaī kari kirpaa saadhu milaavai
nānak saanti hovai man antari nit hiradai hari guṇ gaavai.

5. Ram namu

The name of Ram is a jewel hidden in a granary in the stronghold of a mountain!

We got a good teacher so that we could discover this radiant jewel!

We met the sages of Madhav and at sight all sins have been destroyed and we have become extremely pure!

But we also saw five thieves in the city who could make this wealth of Ram's name vanish!

Thanks to the advice of the teacher, the captured wealth
was got released!

O Mother! the mind was emptied by removing the burden of sin!

We attained the primal forefather!

The Lord of the universe has shown mercy so that we could meet good sages!

If Nanak is inside the heart, the heart will always sing of the glory of God (Hari)!

राग : भैरव Rāga : Bhairav

6. हरि का संतु हरि की हार मूरात जिसु हिरदै हरि नामु मुरारि॥
मसतकि भागु होवै जिसू लिखिआ॥
सो गुरमति हिरिदै हरि नामु सम्हारि॥
मधुसूदनु जपीऐ उर धारि॥
देही नगरि तसकर पंच धातू गुर सबदी हरि काढे भारि॥
जिन का हरि सेती मनु मानिआ तिन कारज हरि आपि सवारि॥
तिन चूकी मुहताजी लोकन की हरि अंगीकौरु कीआ करतारि॥
मता मसूरति तां किछु कीजै जे किछु होवै हरि बाहरि॥
जो किछु करे सोई भल होसी हरि धिआवहू अनदिनु नामु मुरारि॥
हरि जो किछु करे सु आपे आपे ओहु पूछि न किसै करे बीचारि॥
नानक सो प्रभु सदा धिआईऐ जिनि मेलिआ सतिगुरु किरपा धारि॥

hari kā santu hari kī hār mūrāt jisu hiradai hari nāmu murāri

mastaki bhāgu hovai jisū likhiaa

so gurmati hiridai hari nāmu samhāri

madhusūdanu japīai ur dhāri

dehī nagari taskar panc dhātū gur sabdī hari kaaḍhe bhāri

jin kā hari setī manu māniaa tin kāraj hari aapi savāri

tin cūkī muhtājī lokan kī hari angeekauru kīaa kartāri

matā masūrati tam kicchu kījai je kicchu hovai hari bāhari

jo kicchu kare soī bhal hosī hari dhiaavahū anadinu nāmu murāri

hari jo kicchu kare su aape aape ohu poocchi na kisai kare bīcāri

nānak so prabhu sadā dhiaaīai jini meliaa satiguru kirpa dhāri.

6. Hari ka santu

They who have in their hearts the name of Hari, the form of Hari and the devotees of Hari,
will have good fortune written on their heads!
Hence following the advice of the teacher, hold in your hearts the name of Hari!
Clasp *Madhusudan* to your heart and chant his name!
Through the word of the teacher, Hari will destroy the five thieves (five senses) in the city of the body!
He whose heart is united with the name of Hari, his tasks will be accomplished speedily!
He who accepts Hari as the master will have no want or poverty!
Hari will keep away all acts of conspiracy and diseases!
If every day Murari's name is meditated upon, whatever is done will be for the good!
Hari does things on His own. He does not have to ask anyone or consult anyone!
Always think of guru Nanak, who is full of compassion.

राग : मारु Rāga : Māru

7. हरि हरि भगति भरे भंडारा॥ गुरमुखि रामु करे निसतारा॥
जिस नो क्रिपा करे मेरा सुआमी सो हरि के गुण गावै जीउ॥
हरि हरि क्रिपा करे बनवाली॥ हरि हिरदै सदा सदा समाली॥
हरि हरि नामु जपहु मेरे जीअड़े जपि हरि हरि नामु छडावै जीउ॥
सुख सागरु अंम्रितु हरि नाउ॥ मंगत जनु जाचै हरि देहु पसाउ॥
हरि सति सति सदा हरि सति हरि सति मैरै मनि भावै जीउ॥
नवे छिद्र स्रवहि अपवित्रा॥ बोलि हरि नाम पवित्र सभि किता॥
जे हरि सुप्रसंनु होवै मेरा सुआमी हरि सिमरत मलु लहि जावै जीउ॥
माइआ मोहु बिखमु है भारी॥ किउ तरीअै दुतरु संसारी॥
सतिगुरु बोहिथु देइ प्रभु साचा जपि हरि हरि पारि लंघावै जीउ॥
तू सरबत्र तेरा सभु कोई॥ जो तू करहि सोई प्रभ होई॥
जनु नानकु गुण गावै बेचारा हरि भावै हरि थाइ पावै जीउ॥

hari hari bhagati bhare bhandārā gurmukhi rāmu kare nistārā
jis no kripa kare merā suaamī so hari ke guṇ gāvai jeeu
hari hari kripa kare banvālī hari hiradai sadā sadā samālī
hari hari nāmu japhu mere jeeaḍe japi hari hari nāmu chaḍāvai jeeu
sukh sāguru amritu hari naau mangat janu jaacai hari dehu pasaau
hari sati sati sadā hari sati hari sati merai mani bhaavai jīu
nave chidr sravahi apavitrā boli hari nām pavitr sabhi kitā
je hari suprasannu hovai merā suāmī hari simarat malu lahi jāvai jeeu
maaiaa mohu bikhamu hai bhaarī kiu tarīai dutaru samsārī
satiguru bohithu dei prabhu saacaa japi hari hari paari langhaavai jeeu
tū sarbatr terā sabhu koī jo tū karhi soī prabh hoī
janu nānaku guṇ gaavai becārā hari bhāvai hari thāi pāvai jīu.

7. Hari hari bhagati

Fill up the reservoir with devotion to Hari!
Through the teacher, Ram will save us!
He, on whom Hari shows mercy, will live singing of the glory of Hari!
Hari, the dweller of the forest, will show mercy. Always keep Hari in the heart!
Let me spend my life reciting the name of Hari!
Hari is the boat in the ambrosial ocean of bliss!
Whatever is asked, Hari gives, pleased!
Hari is the only reality! Let me live thinking of Hari in my mind!
If the name of Hari, is chanted, all impurities and dissensions will be removed.
If my master, Hari is pleased, all impurities will go away!
O Mother! misfortunes are burdensome, how to cross the difficult Samsara?
The good teacher says if Hari's name is chanted, Hari will help cross the ocean of Samsara!
The Lord is everywhere. He is present in whatever we do!
Let us sing of the good qualities of Nanak and meditate on Hari and live a pure life!

राग : श्री Rāga : Śrī

8. गुण गावा गुण विथरा गुण बोली मेरी माइ ॥
गुरमुखि सजणु गुणकारीआ मिलि सजण हरि गुण गाइ ॥
हीरै हीरु मिलि बेधिआ रंगि चलूलै नाइ ॥
मेरे गोविंदा गुण गावा त्रिपति मनि होइ ॥
अंतरि पिआस हरि नाम की गुरु तुसि मिलावै सोइ ॥
मनु रंगहु वडभागीहो गुरु तुठा करे पसाउ ॥
गुरु नामु द्रिड़ाइ रंग सिउ हउ सतिगुर कै बलि जाउ ॥
बिनु सतिगुर हरि नामु न लभई लख कोटी करम कमाउ ॥
बिनु भागा सतिगुरु ना मिलै घरि बैठिआ निकटि नित पासि ॥
सतिगुरु बोहिथु हरि नाव है कितु बिधि चड़िआ जाइ ॥
सतिगुर कै भाणै जो चलै विचि बोहिथ बैठा आइ ॥
धंनु धंनु वडभागी नानका जिना सतिगुरु लए मिलाइ ॥

gunḥ gāvā gunḥ vitharaa gunḥ bolī merī maai
gurmukhi sajaṇu guṇkārīaa mili sajaṇ hari guṇ gaai
hīrai heeru mili bedhiaa rangi calūlai naai
mere govindā guṇ gāvā tripati mani hoi
antari piaas hari nām kī guru tusi milāvai soi
manu rangahu vaḍbhaagīho guru tuṭhaa kare pasaau
guru nāmu driḍaai rang siu hau satigur kai bali jaau
binu satigur hari nāmu na labhaī lakh koṭī karam kamaau
binu bhaagaa satiguru nā milai gharibaiṭhiaa nikaṭi nit paasi
satiguru bohithu hari nāv hai kitu bidhi caḍiyaa jāi
satigur kai bhaaṇai jo calai vici bohith baiṭhaa aai
dhamnu dhamnu vaḍbhaagī nānakā jinā satiguru lai milaai.

8. Gun gava

My Mother!

Let us sing, spread and speak of the glory of God (Hari)!

Through the teacher's mouth, we have met good

people and are singing of the good qualities of Hari!

We got diamonds with piercing colours, but these do not hold the mind permanently!

My mind is only set on singing the glory of my Govind!

The mind thirsts for the name of Hari

When the Teacher is pleased with you, the mind becomes very fortunately enlightened!

The good teacher shows the good way!

Without the good teacher, one does not get the name of

Hari! even if one tries a million times!

Without good luck one does not get the good teacher,

with whom one can sit near, on the carpet.

The teacher teaches that Hari is the boat to cross the

ocean of *samsara.*

It is our very very good fortune that we have got a

teacher like Guru Nanak!

राग : धनाश्री Rāga : Dhanāśrī

9. हरि पड़ु हरि लिखु हरि जपि हरि गाउ हरि भउजलु पारि उतारी॥
मनि बचनि रिदै धिआइ हरि होइ संतुसटु इब भणु हरि नामु मुरारी॥
मनि जपीऐ हरि जगदीस मिली संगति साधू मीत॥
सदा अंनदु होवै दिनु राती हरि कीरति करि बनवारी॥
हरि हरि करी द्रिसटि तब भइओ मनि उदमु हरि हरि नामु जपिओ गति भई हमारी॥
जन नानक की पति राखु मेरे सुआमी हरि आइ परिओ है सरणि तुमारी॥

hari paḍu hari likhu hari japi hari gaau hari bhaujalu pāri utaarī
mani bacani ridai dhiaai hari hoi santusaṭu iba bhaṇu hari nāmu murārī
mani japīai hari jagdees milī sangati sādhū meet
sadaa anandu hovai dinu rātī hari keerati kari banavaarī
hari hari karī drisaṭi tab bhaio mani udamu hari hari nāmu japio gati bhaī hamārī
jan nānak kī pati raakhu mere suaamī hari aai pario hai saraṇi tumaarī.

9. Hari padu

Read about Hari! Write about Hari! Chant the name of Hari!
Sing of Hari! Worship Hari and cross the ocean of Samsara!
In mind and word, think only of Hari and be happy!
The name of Hari who is also *Murāri* confers happiness!
Chant in the mind the name of Hari, the Lord of universe!
Meet with and seek the sweet company of sages!
Always be happy, day and night reciting the name of Hari, who is Krishna, the wanderer of forests!
Keep Hari in the mind, he is the real friend!
Chant the name of Hari! He is our goal, our friend!
O Lord of Nanak! Protect me, who is following the path shown by Guru Nanak!

राग : देवगान्धारि Rāga : Devagāndhāri

10. हरि गुण गावै हउ तिसु बलिहारी ॥
देखि देखि जीवा साध गुर दरसनु जिस हिरदै नामु मुरारी ॥
तुम पवित्र पावन पुरख प्रभ सुआमी हम किउ करि मिलह जूठारी ॥
हमरै जीइ होरु मुखि होरु होत है हम करमहीण कूड़िआरी ॥
हमरी मुद्र नामु हरि सुआमी रिद अंतरि दुसट दुसटारी ॥
जिउ भावै तिउ राखहु सुआमी जन नानक सरणि तुम्हारी ॥

hari guṇ gaavai hau tisu balihārī
dekhi dekhi geevaa saadh gur darsanu jis hiradai naamu murārī
tum pavitr paavan purakh prabh suaamī ham kiu kari milah jooṭhaaree
hamarai jeei horu mukhi horu hot hai ham karamheeṇ kūḍiaarī
hamarī mudr nāmu hari suaamī rid antari dusaṭ dusṭaarī
jiu bhaavai tiu raakhhu suaamī jan nānak saraṇi tumhārī.

10. Harigun gāvai

I sing of the good qualities of Hari!
I am His devotee!
See! all my life I have thirsted to see the Guru,
in whose heart dwells the name of Murari!
You are pure, sacred, complete radiant Lord!
I have done impure things!
We are sinners with bad Karma!
Our lives are not turned towards you!
Our trade name is Lord Hari!
Please empty our minds of all evil!
O Lord! Please do whatever you deem fit!
We follow the path shown by Guru Nanak!

SONGS OF RAHIM

Song	*Raga*
1. Chabi aavan mohanlalki	Suddhakalyana
2. Pat chaahe tan	Jhanjhauti
3. Kamaldalnainaniki	Patamanjari
4. Sarad nisi niseethe	Chandni Kedara
5. Kalit lalit maalaa	Lalat
6. Drig cchakit cchabeelee	Deś
7. Kathin kutil kaalee	Huseni
8. Jarad basanvaalaa	Bagesree
9. Taral taranisee hai	Malkauns
10. Bhujag jug kidhau hai	Bilawal

RAHIM

RAHIM (16th Century A.D.)

Rahim, whose full name was Nawab Abdur-Rahim Khan-i-khanan, was a poet in Emperor Akbar's court.

He was a scholar well versed in Persian, Arabic, Turkish, Sanskrit, Braj Bhasha and Avadhi.

He was a contemporary of Tulsidas.

Rahim's obsession was the amorous sports of Lord Krishna with the Gopis.

Like Surdas, Rahim expresses, in a few couplets, the yearning of forlorn Gopis for union with Krishna and in others the bliss of meeting with Krishna.

The radiant beauty of *Srinathji* lured the Pathan Rahim and made him as lovelorn as the Gopis of Brindavan.

In one couplet, Rahim exclaims:

> "*The eyes are all too full of Mohan's beauty*
> *How can there be room for other beauties?*
> *Find the caravansarai full, every new*
> *traveller turns away from the gates.*"

Passionate love, powerful imagery, an outstanding literary acumen and a deep knowledge of the myths and legends of India enabled Rahim to pour out in beautiful *Brij Bhasha* lyrics that elevate us to ecstatic heights of spiritual experience.

राग : शुद्धकल्याण Rāga : Śuddhakalyāṇa

1. छबि आवन मोहनलालकी।
काछिनि काछे कलित मुरलि कर पीत पिछौरी सालकी॥

बंक तिलक केसरकौ कीनें, दुति मानों बिधु बालकी।
बिसरत नाहि सखी, मो मनतें, चितवन नयन बिसालकी॥

नीकी हँसनि अधर सुधरनिकी, छबि छीनी सुमन गुलालकी।
जलसों डारि दियों पुरइन पर, डोलनि मुकता-मालकी॥

आप मोल बिन मोलनि डोलनि, बोलनि मदनगोपालकी।
यह सुरूप निरखै सोइ जानै, या 'रहीम' के हालकी॥

chabi aavan mohanlālkī
kaachini kaache kalit murali kar peet pichaurī saalkī
bank tilak kesarkau keenem, duti maano bidhu baalakī
bisarat naahi sakhī, mo mantem, citavan nayan bisaalkī
neekee hansani adhar sudharniki, chabi cheenee suman gulālkī
jalson ḍaari diyon purin par, ḍolni muktā-mālkī
aap mol bin molni ḍolni, bolni madangopālkī
yah surūp nirkhai soi jaanai, yaa rahīm ke haalkī.

1. Chabi avan mohanlalki

A portrait of Krishna the charmer's coming:
A tightly worn loin cloth, flute in hand, wearing a yellow shawl made from the Sal tree!
An auspicious mark of *keśar* on the forehead!
Radiant like the young moon!
Don't forget, friend! the wide eyes which steal your heart!
the innocent smile on the nectar-like lips!
looking like the full blown rose!
Sitting on the lotus!
the pearl necklace swings!
How can you value the sweet words of Madana Gopal?
I only know this: I keep looking at this beautiful form!
This is Rahim's condition!

राग : झँझौटी Rāga : Jhanjhauṭī

2. पट चाहै तन, पेट चाहत छदन मन,
चाहत है, धन जेती सम्पदा सराहिबी।
तेरोई कहायकै, रहीम कहै दीनबन्धु,
आपनी बिपत्ति जाय काके द्वार काहिबी?
पेट भरि खायो चाहै, उद्यम बनायौ चाहै,
कुटुँब जियायो चाहै, काढ़ि गुन लाहिबी।
जीविका हमारी जोपै औरनके कर डारौ,
ब्रजके बिहारी! तो तिहारी कहाँ साहिबी॥

paṭ caahai tan, peṭ caahat chadan man,
caahat hai, dhan jetī sampadaa saraahibee
teroī kahaayakai, rahīm kahai deenabandhu,
aapanee bipatti jaay kaake dvaar kaahibee?
peṭ bhari khaayo cāhai, udyam banāyau cāhai,
kuṭumb jiyāyo cāhai, kaaḍhi gun lāhibī
jeevikā hamārī jopai auranke kar ḍaarau
braj ke bihārī! to tihārī kahaan saahibee.

2. Pat cahe tan

You say:
Have as much cloth as the body wants!
Whatever the stomach wants!
Have wealth and wine as much as you want!
Rahim says: O Lord of the distressed!
Why do you show the way to trouble?
We can eat stomachful!
We can have a family
If our life is surrendered to someone else,
O wanderer of Brindavan! Where is your dominant rule?

राग : पटमञ्जरी Rāga : Paṭamanjarī

3. कमलदल नैननिकी उनमानि।
बिसरत नाहि सखी, मो मनतें मन्द-मन्द मुसुकानि॥

यह दसननि दुति चपलाहूतें महाचपल चमकानि।
बसुधाकी बस करी मधुरता, सुधा-पगी बतरानि॥

चढ़ी रहै चित उर बिसालकी, मुकुत माल थहरानि।
नृत्य-समय पीताम्बरहूकी, फहरि-फहरि फहरानि।

अनुदिन श्रीबृंदाबन ब्रजते, आवन आवन जानि।
अब 'रहीम' चिततें न टरति है, सकल स्यामकी बानि॥

kamaldal nainanikī unmānī
bisarat naahi sakhī, mo mantem mand mand musukāni
yah dasnani duti capalāhūte mahācapal camakāni
vasudhākī bas karī madhuratā, sudhā-pagī batarāni
caḍhī rahai cit ur bisālkī, mukut māl thaharāni
nṛtya-samay pītāmbarhūkī, phahari-phahari phaharāni
anudin śrībrindāvan brajate, aavan aavan jāni
ab rahīm citte na ṭarati hai, sakal syāmkī bāni.

3. Kamaldal nainanki

A depiction of the lotus-eyed Lord!
Don't forget, friend! the slow gentle smile!
The radiance of this vision is so fleeting and effulgent!
Stay on the earth is made sweet!
Sweet talk exudes nectar-like charm!
The pearl necklace swings!
At the time of dance, the yellow *pitambara* garment flies and flies!
Now Rahim's mind does not waver! It is filled with the dark-hued Krishna's image!

राग : चांदनी केदारा Rāga : Chāndnī Kedārā

4. शरद-निशि-निशथे चाँदकी रोशनाई।
सघन-बन-निकुञ्जे कान्ह बंसी बजाई॥
रति, पति, सुत, निद्रा साइयाँ छोड़ भागी,
मदन-शिरसि भूयः क्या बला आन लागी॥

śarad-niśi-niśthe cāndkī rośanāī
saghan-ban-nikunje kanh bansī bajāī
rati, pati, sut, nidrā sāiyān cchoḍ bhāgī
madan-śirasi bhūyaḥ kyā balā aan lāgī.

4. Sarad nisi

In the autumnal night there is radiant moonlight!
In the thick forest bower, Krishna is playing the flute!
I gave up beloved, husband, children, sleep, everything and ran!
When Cupid rules the head, where is modesty?

राग : ललत Rāga : Lalat

5. कलित ललित माला वा जवाहर जड़ा था,
चपल चखनवाला चाँदनीमें खड़ा था।
कटि-तट-बिच मेला पीत सेला नवेला,
अलिबन अलबेला यार मेरा अकेला॥

kalit lalit mālā vā javāhar jaḍā thā
capal cakhanvālā cāndnīmem khaḍā thā
kaṭi-taṭ-bic melā pīt selā navelā
aliban albelā yār merā akelā.

5. Kalit lalit

His lovely garland was made of jewels!
The restless beloved was standing in the moonlight!
He was wearing on his waist a lovely yellow scarf!
My handsome lover was alone in the cuckoo forest!

राग : देश Rāga : Desh

6. दृग छकित छबीली छेलराकी छरी थी,
मणि-जटित रसीली माधुरी मूँदरी थी।
अमल कमल ऐसा खूबसे खूब देखा,
कहि न सकी जैसा श्यामका हस्त देखा॥

drg chakit chabīlī chelrākī charī thī
maṇi-jaṭit rasīlī mādhurī mūndarī thī
amal kamal eisā khoobse khoob dekhā
kahin na sakī jaisā śyāmkā hast dekhā.

6. Dṛg cchakit

Nowhere can one see a hand like Krishna's!
It is like pure lotus flower!
There is a beautiful ring made of jewels in it!
It is so graceful that the eyes tremble on looking at it!

राग : हुसेनि | Rāga : Huseni

7. कठिन कुटिल काली देख दिलदार जुलफें,
अलि–कलित बिहारी आपने जीकी कुलफें।
सकल शशि–कलाको रोशनी–हीन लेखौं,
अहह ब्रजलल्लाको किस तरह फेर देखौं॥

kaṭhin kuṭil kālī dekh dildār julphen
ali-kalit bihārī āpne jīkī kulphen
sakal śaśi-kalāko rośanī-heen lekhaun
ahah brajlalaako kis tarah pher dekhaun.

7. Kathin kutil

The hair locks are curly, dark and ravish the heart!
Krishna sporting with his female friends pleases the heart!
All the moon's rays are lustreless,
When one sees the sport of the Darling of Brindavan!

राग : बागेश्री

Rāga : Bāgeśrī

8. जरद बसनवाला गुलचमन देखता था,
झुक-झुक मतवाला गावता रेखता था।
श्रुति युग चपलासे कुण्डलें झूमते थे,
नयन कर तमाशे मस्त ह्वै घूमते थे॥

jarad basanvālā gulcaman dekhtā thā
jhuk-jhuk matwālā gāvtā rekhtā thā
śruti yug capalaase kuṇḍlen jhoomte the
nayan kar tamāśe mast hvain ghoomte the.

8. Jarad basanwala

    The One with the yellow garment was looking at the flower garden!
    The intoxicated One was bending and bending and singing and dancing!
    With the movement of keeping rhythm, the ear ornaments were swinging!
    Making fun with the eyes, he was wandering joyously!

राग : मालकौंस

Rāga : Mālkauns

9. तरल तरनि-सी हैं तीर-सी नोकदारैं,
अमल कमल-सी हैं दीर्घ हैं बिल बिदारैं।
मधुर मधुप हेरैं माल मस्ती न राखैं,
बिलसति मन मेरे सुन्दरी स्याम आँखें॥

taral tarni-sī hain tīr-sī nokdaarain
amal kamal-sī hain deergh hain bil bidaarain
madhur madhup herain māl mastī na rākhain
bilsati man mere sundarī syām aankhen.

9. Taral taranisi

Sparkling like the sun, pointed like the arrow!
Pure like the lotus and long and deep like a hole!
They have the sweetness of nectar, without any pride of possession!
The beautiful eyes of dark-hued Krishna!
My heart delights in them!

राग : बिलावल् Rāga : Bilāwal

10. भुजग जुग किधौं हैं काम कमनैत सोहैं,
नटवर! तव मोहैं बाँकुरी मान भौंहैं।
सुनु सखि, मृदु बानी बेदुरुस्ती अकिलमें,
सरल-सरल सानी कै गई सार दिलमें॥

bhujag jug kidhaun hain kām kamnait sohain
naṭwar! tava mohain bānkurī mān bhaunhain
sunu sakhi, mṛdu bānī bedurustī akilmen
saral-saral sānī kai gayee sār dilmen.

10. Bhujag jug

The pair of arms is like Cupid's bow!
O skilful Dancer! Your bold eyebrows are captivating!
Listen, friend! soft speech, there is no discordant note anywhere!
the whole heart has become soft and tender for Him.

SONGS OF APPAYYA DIKSHITAR

Song	*Raga*
1. Naham roddhum karananicayam	Hamsadhwani
2. Kshamasyeva tvamiha karunasagarah	Sankarabharanam
3. Pranotkranti vyatikaradalatsandhibandhe	Kamboji
4. Adyaiva tvatpadanalinayor	Suddha Dhanyasi
5. Dasosmiti tvayi sivamaya	Mohanam
6. Karmajnana pracayamakhilam	Hindolam
7. Ekosi tvam siva	Todi
8. Sarvajnastva niravadhikrpasagarah	Suddhasaveri
9. Sarvam sadasiva sahasva	Sri
10. Sambho mahadeva deva	Ragamalika

APPAYYADIKSHITAR

APPAYYA DIKSHITAR (16th-17th Century A.D.)

Sri Appayya Dikshitar, the renowned scholar and mystic poet philosopher of South India, probably lived in the 16th-17th century A.D.

He was born in the village of *Adayappalam*, near *Virinchipuram*, Kanchi, in a family of philosophical and devotional poets. Appayya, a born devotee of Lord Siva, considered *Bhakti* or devotion and the resultant grace of God as indispensable for ultimate liberation.

Like many other mystic saints, Appayya had misgivings about his own devotion to God and wanted to test the strength of his devotion. He hence drank the maddening juice of *Kanakaphala* and in a delirious state poured out fifty devotional songs, which were taken down by his disciples. These fifty verses constitute the famous *Ātmarpana Stuti* (lit. song of self-surrender), selections from which are included in this volume.

As can be seen, these songs are soaked in the deepest devotion and seek God's help in crossing the abyss of the phenomenal world.

Also included is Appayya Dikshitar's famous *Mārgabandhustotram*, in which the Lord is deemed the friend on the road. This prayer is usually recited on commencement of journeys for a safe and trouble-free arrival at the destination.

Appayya Dikshitar implies that the Lord's guidance is required not only for earthly journeys but also on the spiritual path to salvation.

राग : हंसध्वनि

Rāga : Hamsadhwani

1. नाहं रोद्धुं करणनिचयं दुर्नयं पारयामि
स्मारं स्मारं जनिपथरुजं नाथ सीदामि भीत्या।
किं वा कुर्वे किमुचितमिह क्वाद्यगच्छामि हन्त
त्वत्पादाब्जप्रपदनमृते नैव पश्याम्युपायम्॥

naaham roddhum karaṇanicayam durnayam paarayaami
smaaram smaaram janipatharujam naatha seedaami bheetyaa
kim vā kurve kimucitamiha kvaadya gacchaami hanta
tvatpaadaabja prapadanamṛte naiva paśyaamyupaayam.

1. Naham roddhum karananicayam

O Lord!

I am unable to control the group of senses, which are diffucult to subdue.

Thinking of the sorrow inherent in the path from birth to death, I tremble.

What can I do? I do not know what is the appropriate course of action. Where can I go?

Other than falling at your lotus feet and seeking refuge, I do not know any other way.

राग : शंकराभरणं Rāga : Śankarābharaṇam

2. क्षाम्यस्येव त्वमिह करुणासागरः कृत्स्नमागः
संसारोत्थं गिरिश सभयप्रार्थनादैन्यमात्रात्।
यद्यप्येवं प्रतिकलमहं व्यक्तमागस्सहस्रं
कुर्वन्मूकः कथमिव तथा निरतृपः प्रार्थयेयम्॥

kshaamyasyeva tvamiha karuṇaasaagaraḥ kṛstnamaagaḥ
samsaarottham giriśa sabhayapraarthanaadainyamaatraat
yadyapyevam pratikalamaham vyakta maagassahasram
kurvanmookaḥ kathamiva tathaa niratṛpaḥ praarthayeyam.

2. Kshamasyeva tvamiha

O Lord who reside in the mountains!
Being an ocean of mercy, you pardon all my sins of this phenomenal life, because of my pitiable pleas made in fear.
In spite of this, every moment I commit thousands of sins deliberately.

राग : कांबोजि

Rāga : Kāmboji

3. प्राणोत्क्रान्ति व्यतिकरदलत्सन्धिबन्धे शरीरे
प्रेमावेशप्रसरदमिताक्रन्दिते बन्धुवर्गे।
अन्तः प्रज्ञामपि शिव भजन्नन्तरायैरनन्तैः
आविद्धोहं त्वयि कथमिमामर्पयिष्यामि बुद्धिम्॥

praaṇotkraanti vyatikaradalatsandhibandhe śareere
premaaveśaprasaradamitaakrandite bandhuvarge
antaḥ prajnaamapi śiva bhajannantaraayairanantaiḥ
aaviddhoham tvayi kathamimāmarpayishyaami buddhim.

3. Prānotkrānti

O Auspicious One!
When the life breath leaves the body and consequently
the various linkages disappear,
and the group of relatives cry excessively, out of love,
Though fully aware of the proximity of death,
trammelled by myriad bottlenecks,
How do I submit this mind of mine to you?

राग : शुद्ध धन्यासि Rāga : Śuddha Dhanyāsi

4. अद्यैव त्वत्पदनलिनयोरर्पयाम्यन्तरात्मन्
आत्मानम्मे सहपरिकरैरद्रिकन्याधिनाथ।
नाहं बोद्धुं शिव तव पदन्न क्रियायोगचर्याः
कर्तुं शक्नोम्यनितरगतिः केवलं त्वां प्रपद्ये॥

adyaiva tvatpadanalinayorarpayaamyantaraatman
aatmaanamme sahaparikarairadrikanyaadhinaatha
naaham boddhum śiva tava padanna kriyaayogacaryaaḥ
kartum śaknomyanitaragatiḥ kevalam tvaam prapadye.

4. Adyaiva

O Lord who reside in the lotus of my heart!
I offer myself with all the accompaniments (mind, senses, breath, etc.) now itself at your lotus feet.
O Lord of the mountain-daughter!
O Auspicious One!
I am not competent enough to follow the path of Yogic practices and other rites to understand your form!
Having no other way, I seek refuge in you.

राग : मोहनं

Rāga : Mohanam

5. दासोस्मीति त्वयिशिवमया नित्यसिद्धं निवेद्यं
जानास्येतत्त्वमपि यदहं निर्गतिस्संभ्रमामि।
नास्त्येवात्मन्मम किमपि ते नाथ विज्ञापनीयं
कारुण्यान्मे शरणवरणं दीनवृत्तेर्गृहाण॥

daasosmeeti tvayiśivamayaa nityasiddham nivedyam
jaanaasyetattvamapi yadaham nirgatissambhramaami
naastyevaatmanmama kimapi te naatha vijnaapaneeyam
kaaruṇyaanme śaraṇavaraṇam deenavṛttergṛhaaṇa.

5. Dasosmiti

O Auspicious Lord!

The obvious truth that before you, I am a servant

needs to be made known to you by me.

But you already know about it.

You also know that I am wandering aimlessly!

O Master!

There is nothing else that I have to make known to you.

Kindly, out of compassion, accept the plea for refuge

of this destitute.

राग : हिन्दोलं Rāga : Hindolam

6. कर्मज्ञानप्रचयमखिलं दुष्करं नाथ पश्यन्
पापासक्तं हृदयमपि चापारयन्सन्निरोद्धुम्।
संसाराख्ये पुरहर महत्यन्धकूपे विषीदन्
हस्तालंबप्रपतनमिदं प्राप्यते निर्भयोस्मि॥

karmajnaanapracayamakhilam dushkaram naatha paśyan
paapaasaktam hṛdayamapi caapaarayansanniroddhum
samsaaraakhye purahara mahatyandhakoope visheedan
hastaalambaprapatanamidam praapyate nirbhayosmi.

6. Karmajnana pracayamakhilam

O Lord!

I see that practice of *Karma Yoga, Jnāna Yoga* etc. is difficult.

I am also unable to control my mind addicted to sin.

O Destroyer of Tripura!

Though I am sad that I am in this blind well
of the phenomenal world,
I feel fearless holding this hand of yours which you
have let down for me to hold!

राग : तोडि Rāga : Toḍi

7. एकोसि त्वं शिव जनिमतामीश्वरो बन्धमुक्त्योः
क्लेशां गारावलिषु लुठतः कागतिस्त्वांविना मे।
तस्मादस्मिन्नपि पशुपते घोर जन्म प्रवाहे
खिन्नं दैन्याकरमतिभयं मां भजस्व प्रपन्नम्॥

ekosi tvam śiva janimataameeśvaro bandhamuktyoḥ
kleśaam gaaraavalishu luṭhataḥ kaagatistvaamvinaa me
tasmaadasminnapi paśupate ghora janma pravaahe
khinnam dainyaakaramatibhayam maam bhajasva prapannam.

7. Eko asi tvam

O Auspicious Lord!

You control the bondage and liberation of all creatures.

You are the only one to do this.

For me, rolling in the shadows of afflictions

Other than you, where is the refuge?

O Lord of creatures!

Please accept me, who has approached you,

pitiable and highly fearful, having fallen into this

terrible torrent which is birth.

राग : शुद्धसावेरि Rāga : Śuddhasāveri

8. सर्वज्ञस्त्वं निरवधिकृपासागरः पूर्णशक्तिः
कस्मादेनं न गणयसि मामापदब्धौ निमग्नम्।
एकं पापात्मकमपिरुजा सर्वतोऽत्यन्तदीनं
जन्तुं यद्युद्धरसि शिव कस्तावताऽतिप्रसंगः॥

sarvajnastvam niravadhikṛpaasaagaraḥ poorṇaśaktiḥ
kasmaadenam na gaṇayasi maamaapadabdhau nimagnam
ekam paapaatmakamapirujaa sarvatoatyantadeenam
jantum yadyuddharasi śiva kastaavataatiprasangaḥ.

8. Sarvajnastvam

O Auspicious One!
You are omniscient!
You are the ocean of infinite mercy!
You have total power with you!
Why are you ignoring me, fallen into this sea of afflictions?
By rescuing this one creature which is me,
who is a sinner, tormented by sorrow and highly pitiable,
How do you exceed any limits?

राग : श्री

Rāga : Śrī

9. सर्वं सदाशिव सहस्व ममापराधं
मग्नं समुद्धर महत्यमुमापदब्धौ।
सर्वात्मना तव पदांबुजमेव दीनः
स्वामिन्ननन्यशरणः शरणं प्रपद्ये॥

sarvam sadaaśiva sahasva mamaaparaadham
magnam samuddhara mahatyamumaapadabdhau
sarvaatmanaa tava padaambujameva deenaḥ
svaaminnananyaśaraṇaḥ śaraṇam prapadye.

9. Sarvam sadasiva

O ever-auspicious Lord!
Bear with all my faults.

You have to protect this poor soul
fallen into this great abyss of afflictions.

O Master!

I, the pitiable one, having no other refuge,
seek refuge in your lotus feet, surrendering totally.

मार्गबन्धु स्तोत्रं

राग : हंसध्वनि Rāga : Hamsadhwani

10. शंभो महादेव देव
शिव शंभो महादेव देवेश शम्भो
शंभो महादेव देव।

śambho mahaadeva deva
śiva śambho mahaadeva deveśa śambho
śambho mahaadeva deva.

फालावनम्रत्किरीटं
कालनेत्रार्चिषा दग्धपञ्चेषुकीटम्
शूलहतारातिकूटं
शुद्धमर्धेन्दुचूडं भजे मार्गबन्धुम्।

phaalaavanamratkireeṭam
kaalanetraarcishaa dagdhapanceshukeeṭam
śoolahataaraatikooṭam
śuddhamardhenducoodam bhaje maargabandhum.

MĀRGABANDHU STOTRAM

10. Sambho mahadeva deva

O Creator of bliss! O Great Lord! O Lord!

O Auspicious One! Creator of bliss! O Great Lord!

O God of gods!

O Creator of bliss! O Great Lord! O Lord!

I worship the friend of the road,

Who wears on his forehead an unbent crown!

Who burnt Cupid (who has five arrows) with the fire from his fiery eye!

Who slays hordes of enemies with his trident!

And who wears as his crest the pure half moon.

राग : हंसध्वनि Rāga : Hamsadhwani

अङ्गे विराजद्भुजङ्गम्
अभ्रगङ्गातरङ्गाभिरामोत्तमाङ्गम्
ओंकार वाटीकुरङ्गं
सिद्धसंसेविताङ्घ्रिं भजे मार्गबन्धुम्।

ange viraajadbhujangam
abhragangaatarangaabhiraamottamaangam
omkaara vaaṭeekurangam
siddhasamsevitaanghrim bhaje maargabandhum.

नित्यं चिदानन्दरूपं
निहनुताशेषलोकेशवैरिप्रतापम्
कार्तस्वरागेन्द्रचापं
कृत्तिवासं भजे दिव्यसन्मार्गबन्धुम्।

nityam cidaanandarūpam
nihnutaaśeshalokeśavairiprataapam
kaartasvaraagendracaapam
kṛttivaasam bhaje divya sanmaargabandhum.

Serpents adorn his body!

Waves of the flowing Ganga embellish his head!

He is the deer in the garden of Om, the pranava sound!

His feet are worshipped by the Siddhas!

I worship the divine friend of the good road,

Who is ever the embodiment of Consciousness-bliss,

Who has the power and glory, as the Lord of the universe, of extinguishing enemies without a trace,

Who has as his bow the golden mountain!

and who wears the elephant skin as his dress!

राग : मध्यमावति Rāga : Madhyamāvati

कन्दर्पदर्पघ्नमीशं
कालकण्ठं महेशं महाव्योमकेशम्
कुन्दाभदन्तं सुरेशं
कोटिसूर्यप्रकाशं भजे मार्गबन्धुम्।

kandarpadarpaghnameeśam
kaalakaṇṭham maheśam mahaavyomakeśam
kundaabhadantam sureśam
koṭisūryaprakaaśam bhaje maargabandhum.

मन्दार भूतेरुदारं
मन्थरागेन्द्रसारं महागौर्यदूरं
सिन्धूरदूरप्रचारं
सिन्धुराजातिधीरं भजे मार्गबन्धुम्।

mandaarabhūterudaaram
mantharaagendrasaaram mahaagauryadooram
sindhūradūrapracaaram
sindhuraajaatidheeram bhaje maargabandhum.

I worship that friend of the road,
the Lord who destroyed the arrogance of Cupid,
Who wears poison in his throat,
the great Lord whose hair is the ether,
Whose teeth shine like white jasmine,
the Lord of the angels,
whose radiance is that of ten million suns!

I worship the friend of the road,
Who is more giving than the wish-granting Kalpa tree
Who is stronger than the Mandhara mountain,
Who is never far away from the fair goddess, *Gauri*,
Who wanders far on the bull,
Who is more valorous than the ocean king!

SONGS OF BHIMA BHOI

	Song	*Raga*
1.	Pada pani nahim	Meru
2.	Mulasunya gharaku kar vivek	Vasanta
3.	Kehu dekhicha ki beni netrare	Jayajayanti
4.	Rup rekha nahim he	Misramalhar
5.	Daka na suna kimpai	Khamas
6.	Lata vane vuli dekha	Behag
7.	Sunya mandire vihara	Sarfarda
8.	Sthavaru jangama kitaru	Paras
9.	Tahanku jebana jana	Malhar
10.	Aruṇa tarasa padile	Bilawal

BHIMA BHOI

BHIMA BHOI (1849 A.D.-1894 A.D.)

Bhima Bhoi, the blind, tribal mystic of Orissa, is noted for his devotional songs in honour of God, the Unmanifest (*Nikāra* or *Nirguna Brahman*).

The philosophy of Bhima Bhoi, termed "*Mahima Dharma*", extols God as the Unseen Power which pervades everything in the universe.

Bhima Bhoi was born in 1849 in a poor tribal family in the Diha village near Radhakol, Orissa. He was born blind.

Bhima Bhoi did not have any education.

Despite his physical handicap of blindness, Bhima Bhoi became a great poet of devotional songs (locally called *Bhajans*). These were sung by him and written down by his disciples, who popularised them among the people.

The songs have been compiled into a large number of books, chief among them being the *Bṛhat Bhajanamala* and *Stuti Chintamani*, selections from which have been included in this volume.

The followers of *Mahima Dharma* established by Bhima Bhoi could either be celibates or householders. Bhima Bhoi himself was a householder, having married a Brahmin girl named Annapurna, who bore him two children: a son named Kapileswar and a daughter named Labanybati. Bhima Bhoi died in 1894 at the age of 45.

Adoration of God as an invisible presence is unique in the Bhakti movement in India, where the other mystics poured out their love for specific manifestations of Divinity.

Bhima Bhoi's songs reveal a passionate yearning for God, the Invisible, Elusive One.

राग : मेरु Rāga : Meru

1. पादपाणि नहीं तङ्कु धरीबा किये?
एमन्त ब्रह्मस्वरूप देखा न ययेे।
नहीं तङ्क पेट अन्त फिटाई कहुच्छि गोता;
नर देह वही तङ्कु कलिबा नुहे।
तङ्क पारि शान्ति पाणे, त्रिभुवने नहीं जाने;
निन्दा स्तुति हानि लाभ सकल सहे।

भक्षण नहीं आहार, रज वीरयरु बाहरा;
क्षुधा तृषा कले क्षीर नीर न पीये।
न लगाई अङ्गे धूलि, विराजि दिशन्ति झालि;
निद्रा घुमाईले उभा आसने सोए।

इच्छारे आसन्ति ब्रह्मि, भकत भावकु प्रेमी;
सुनि चाहिम्बकु कर्ण चक्षु न थाई।
नहीं मुख जिहवा नासा, उत्तर न दिए भासा;
अग पच्छ जनि धीरे समीरे रहे।

pāda pāṇi nahim tanku dharibā kie?
emanta brahma svarūpa dekhā na y(j)ae.

nahim tanka peṭa anta phiṭāī kahucchi gotā;
nara deha vahī tanku kalibā nuhe.
tanka pāri śānti pāṇe, tribhuvane nahim jāne;
nindā stuti hāni lābha sakala sahe.

bhakṣaṇa nahim āhāra, raja vīry(j)aru bāharā;
kṣudhā tṛṣā kale kṣīra nīra na pīe.
na lagāī ange dhūli, virāji diśanti jhāli;
nidrā ghumāīle ubhā āsane soe.

icchāre āsanti brahmi, bhakata bhāvaku premī;
suni chāhimbaku karṇa chakṣu na thāee.
nahīm mukha jihvā nāsā, uttara na die bhāsā;
aga paccha jani dhīre samīre rahe.

1. Pada pani

He has no feet, no hands; who can hold Him?
No one can see His God-form!
He has no stomach, no waist!
No human being can comprehend Him!
There is no one tranquil like Him in all the three worlds!
He can bear blame and praise, profit and loss with equanimity!
He takes no food and is not born out of sexual union!
To quench thirst and hunger he takes no food or water!
Dust cannot pollute Him, He shines radiant!
He enjoys His sleep without lying down!
He appears wherever His devotees seek Him with love!
To hear and see, He has no ears or eyes!
He has no face, tongue or nose, He never answers in words!
He remains, mingling with the breeze!

उलट पलट नोई महा शून्य शून्य देही;
मुख बते जिह्वाकण्ठे बखनि नोही।
सदा जय पूर्णानन्द पैले चर्णे वन्द;
निरन्तरे आज्ञा तिनिपुरे उदये।

नहीं तंक वर्ण चिह्न अशेष रूपरु भिन्न;
सकल धर्म विधान करन्ति न्याये।
असिब जीब होईच्छि, करी सर्व कारौचि;
निष्काम योगरे निज नामाकु थुए।

से ब्रह्मारे तेजझसे, रही न पारुचि पासे;
अनुभवपद मात्र करिचि लये।
कहे भीम सेन भोई, पूर्वादिगे छन्ति रही;
कुह्क सुख जनैबि भेतिले पाये॥

ulaṭa palaṭa noyī, mahā śūnya śūnya dehī;
mukha bate jihvākaṇṭhe bakhani nohee.
sadā jaya purṇānanda paile charṇe vanda;
nirantare ājnā tinipure udaye.

nahīm tanka varṇachihna, aśeṣa rūparu bhinna;
sakala dharma vidhāna karanti nyāye.
asiba y(j)ība hoeecchi, karī sarva kārauchi;
niṣkāma y(j)ogare nija nāmāku thue.

se brahmāre teja jhase, rahi na pāruchi pāse;
anubhava pada mātra karichi laye.
kahe bhīmasena bhoee, pūrvādige chhanti rahī;
kuhka sukha janaibi bhetile pāye.

He does not turn, but moves as the void in the great void!

Mouth and tongue cannot define Him!

Glory to Him! Total bliss flows from Him!

By His command, the three worlds are governed!

He has no colour or sign, He is different from all shapes!

He prescribes all duties!

He does all things!

Hiding Himself in the void, He causes all that happens!

That Godly effulgence makes it impossible to go near Him!

Only in my mind can I feel Him!

Says Bhima, If ever I meet Him

I would tell Him how my life has been spent!

राग : वसन्त Rāga : Vasanta

2. मूल शून्य घरकु कर विवेक।

निःशब्द से भुवन, घु घु नाद गर्जना।
अगाध सागर, नहीं तहीं नीर।
पूरि रहिचि ह्रद पंक।

न पदि पुत बेध, चरि द्वारे खेला।
महा नित्य भूइं, तल तल नहीं।
पदघटे पदुवाचि चमक।

जने जने सुवेव, न थाइ जिन वास।
चौसथि बन्धारे, नृत्य से मन्दिरे।
न बजाई डोला दम तमका॥

mūla sūnya gharaku kara viveka.

niḥśabda se bhuvana, ghu ghu nāda garjanā.
agādha sāgara, nahīṃ tahīṃ nīra.
pūri rahichi hṛada panka.

na padi puta bedha, cari dvāre khelā.
mahā nitya bhūim, tala tala nahīṃ.
padaghaṭe paduvāchi chamaka.

jane jane suveva, na thāi jina vāsa.
chausathi bandhāre, nṛtya se mandire.
na bajāī ḍholā dama tamakā.

2. Mool sunya

Meditate on the primal, empty home in space
where silence reigns and there is a terrible thunder!
The ocean is deep, but there is no water!
The muddy heart is full!

The four doors enclose a non-existent space!

There is sparkle at every footstep!
Everyone is dressed well, but no one has put on a fabric!
There is dance in that home

but no music is heard!

राग : जयजयन्ति

Rāga : Jayajayanti

3. केहु देखिछा कि बेनि नेत्रारे?
बृद्ध वयसारे अतिहि वेशारे
जौथिले एहि पथारे (घोष)।

माता पिता नहीं जन्म होइले
स्तन न चुम्बि न क्षीर खाइले।
बाप धन बोलि गेला करुथिले
पसिथिले मोरा कोलारे।

बधी नहन्ति से सन पिलाटि
वृद्धा होईच्छे जुबा तेजति।
गोरा न दिशन्ति कलिया नुहन्ति
स्वरूपका द्वि मध्यारे॥

kehu dekhichā ki beni netrāre?
bṛddha vayasāre atihi vesāre
y(j)authile ehi pathāre (ghoṣa).

mātā pītā nahīm janma hoile
stana na chumbi na kṣīra khāile.
bāpa dhana boli gelā karuthile
pasithile morā koḷāre.

badhī nahanti se sana pilāṭi,
vṛddhā hoīcche y(j)ubā tejati.
gorā na diśanti kaliyā nuhanti
svarūpakā dvi madhyāre.

3. Kehu dekhicha

Have any of you seen Him with your eyes?
Dressed as a mendicant in old age,
The master passed this way!

He was born with no father and no mother!
He did not suckle his mother's breasts and take milk!

He has played as a small child in my lap

Not that He has grown in age
Only His radiance has grown brighter!
He is neither fair nor dark
somewhere in between!

घरु केभीं नोहिथिले बाहरा,
खजा छुड़ा देई नहीं आहारा।
सुझै गणै नाम देई नहीं,
धूलि खेलुथिले दण्डारे।

रूप वर्ण नहीं झलि दिशन्ति,
पद पाणि नहीं चलुच्छन्ति।
वस्त्र नहीं वृक्ष-बकला पिन्धन्ति,
अदाबन्ध नहीं कटीरे।
मोते धरतीरि आकाश कहिले,
पुत्र योगीन्द्र हेलेनि बोईले।
ब्रह्माण्ड उंधारा करिबे दुमरा,
घोर कलिकाल युगरे।
सर्वशुभे जीवे भेत पवन्ति,
कोले धरी मुखे चुम्ब दियन्ति।
भणे भीम हीन पामर अज्ञान,
लोदुचि ब्रह्माण्ड भितारे॥

gharu kebheem nohithile bāharā,
khajā chuḍā deī nahīm āhārā.
sujhai gaṇai nāma deī nahīm,
dhūli kheluthile daṇḍāre.

rūpa varṇa nahīm jhali diśanti,
pada pāṇi nahīm chalucchanti.
vastra nahīm vṛkṣa-bakalā pindhanti,
adābandha nahīm kaṭīre.

mote dhartīri ākāśa kahile,
putra y(j)ogīndra heleni boīle.
brahmāṇḍa undhārā karibe dumarā,
ghora kalikāla y(j)ugare.

sarva śubhe y(j)eeve bheta pavanti,
kole dharī mukhe chumba diyanti.
bhaṇe bhīma hīna pāmara ajnāna,
loduchi brahmāṇḍa bhitāre.

He never went out of home
I never fed Him, nor gave Him a name!
I did not ask the astrologers to make His horoscope!
He played on the dusty streets!

He has no form or complexion, yet He glows with radiance!
He has no feet or hands, yet He moves!
He has no clothes, He wears a tree bark as loin cloth!

The earth and the sky tell me
that my son is going to be a sage and
that he would redeem us all
in this dark kali yuga.

If ever I could see Him
I would press Him to my bosom and kiss Him,

Says Bhima, the ignorant sinner:
I am looking for Him everywhere in this universe!

राग : मिश्रमल्हार Rāga : Miśramalhār

4. रूप रेखा नहीं है, सून्य देही,
आच्छि उदे होई।
वरसुचि जल न थाई पवना,
अनाचस वायु वहे घन घन।
बधुआचि जल नहीं नदिकुल,
उलुक पटधारा विहि हे।
जक जक ओद सूखिल होइच्छि,
कबत न फितुं नेत्रारे दिशुच्छि।
सेथारे आश्रम अनादित ब्रह्म,
उदे अस्त नहीं तहीं हे।
बलिमति नहीं उबुकुचि ह्रद,
गंगाजल चादि कूपजले गधा।
लभीब मुकति न बुदिब जाति,
पूर्व पुण्य थिले पाई हे॥

rūpa-rekhā nahīṁ he, sūnya dehī,
āchhi ude hoī.

varasuchi jala na thāī pavanā,
anāchasa vāyu vahe ghana ghana.
badhuāchi jala nahīṁ nadikula,
ulukapaṭadhārā vihi he.

jaka jaka oda sukhila hoicchi,
kabata na phitum netrāre diśucchi.
sethāre āśrama anādita brahma,
ude asta nahīṁ tahīṁ he.

balimati nahīṁ ubukuchi hrada,
gangājala chādi kūpajale gadhā.
labhiba mukati na budiba jāti,
pūrva puṇya thile pāī he.

4. Rupa rekha nahim

He has no shape or form!
Formless, he has risen! See!
There is no wind, but it rains and rains!
The breath of life flows fiercely!
The river flows but there is no embankment!
Meteors rain down on the earth!
The drenched earth is now dry
to the eyes!
The doors do not open, but He is revealed!
In the hermitage of God,
there is no sunrise or sunset!
The lake shimmers; there is no sand or earth!
You give up Ganga water and come to the well water!
You will get liberation,
if there is accumulated virtue of previous births!

राग : खमाज़ Rāga : Khamās

5. डाका न सून किं पैं।
भव सिन्धु जले पडि भासु आच्छि मुहीं॥

डाकि डाकि दिव निसि कण्ठ सूखि याई।
जेसने चातक पक्षि तेसनेक मुहीं॥

निरते आसा करिच्छि हृद पद्मे ध्यायी।
किंप निर्दय करुच्छा त्रैलोक्य गोसाइं॥

यर आज्ञारे चलूचि त्रिभुवन मही।
भक्तवत्सल बाण अच्छा परा वाहि॥

मूढ पापि जीव-आत्मा रहिचि किं पै।
के सहू येते कसन मर्त्येदेहवाहि॥

ḍākā na sūna kim paim,
bhava sindhu jale paḍi bhāsu āchhi muhīm.

ḍāki ḍāki diva nisi kaṇṭha sūkhi y(j)āī,
y(j)esane chātaka pakṣi tesaneka muhīm.

nirate āsā karichhi hṛdapadme dhyāyī,
kimpa nirdya karucchā trailokya gosāim.

y(j)ara ājnāre chalūchi tribhuvana mahī,
bhaktavatsala bāṇa achhā parā vāhi.

mūḍha pāpi jīva-ātmā rahichi kim pai,
ke sahū yete kasana martye dehavāhi.

5. Daka na suna

O Lord! I am calling you, why don't you listen?
I float helpless in the ocean of life!

Calling you day and night ceaselessly, my throat has gone dry!

I am like the *chātaka* bird waiting for your rain.

All along I have meditated on you in the lotus of my heart!

Why are you so merciless? O Lord of the three worlds?

At your command, the universe functions!
The flag announcing you as the lover of devotees flutters in the wind.

Why then is the life of this ignorant sinner still there?
Who can bear the anguish in this mortal body?

राग : बेहाग Rāga : Behāg

6. लता वने वुलि देखा बेनिगोति पुष्पा गो।
प्रति दिने तिनिपुरे हीयृच्छन्ति वेसा गो॥

रूप वृक्ष मूले चेर नहीं त विकासा गो।
मेरुकु द्विगुणे मोटा होईचि प्रकासा गो॥

अवसन्ति पल्लबुचि नहीं मधुमासा गो।
निति फुटे निति टूटे न कराई वासा गो॥

latā vane vuli dekhā benigoti puṣpā go,
prati dine tinipure heeycchanti vesā go.

rūpa vṛkṣa mūle chera nahīm ta vikāsā go,
meruku dviguṇe mōṭā hoīchi prakāsā go.

avasanti pallabuchi nahīm madhumāsā go,
niti phuṭe niti ṭūṭe na karāī vāsā go.

6. Lata vane vuli dekha

Walk around in the forest of creepers and see those flowers which are renewed every day in all the three worlds!
See the shape of a tree that has no roots
but has double the thickness of Mount Meru!
It is not spring, yet the tree flowers!
The flowers blossom and fall off without any aroma!

अनाच्छाया तरुतले करिच्छन्ति वास गो।
कधरु पडिले झडे सर्वे यिबे नास गो॥

चारि परकारे रूप वर्णा तर दृश्य गो।
नहीं मधुरसा तहीं तेज तर विस गो॥

चतुर्थ पखुद दुति पखडे विकास गो।
चारि वर्णे रंग भृंग न जाई त पास गो॥

भगत जनक चित्ते हुए अदृस गो।
कहे भीम भोई साधुजन घेन वास गो॥

anācchāyā tarutale karicchanti vāsa go,
kadharu paḍile jhaḍe sarve y(j)ibe nāsa go.

chāri parakāre rūpavarṇā tara dṛśya go,
nahīm madhurasā tahīm teja tara visa go.

chaturtha pakhuda duti pakhaḍe vikāsa go,
chāri varṇe ranga bhṛnga na y(j)āī ta pāsa go.

bhagata janaka chitte huai adṛsa go,
kahe bhīma bhoī sādhujana ghena vāsa go.

Under the shadowless tree they live.
When the buds fall off, they will all be destroyed.

The flowers have four colours.
But there is no honey but only poison in them.
They have four petals which shine.
But the bee of four colours does not go near them.

The flower vanishes in the hearts of devotees.
Says Bhima Bhoi: O pious Ones! relish its fragrance!

राग : सर्‌फार्‌दा Rāga : Sarfārdā

7. सून्य मन्दिरे विहारा, रूपरेखा नहीं जरा।
दुई पद न मिसै एक पद धरा धरा॥

अलेखा पटना पुर, से तबारे तंक घरा।
नहीं सरदा उसुमा साधु जने हेतु करा॥

निरामिस नियन्त पियूथिले लगे मीटा।
अदेखा अनामे स्वदा से सुधा धारा॥

देखि त चातक चली, ज्ञानि मरुच्छन्ति भलि।
चक्षु मतकरु वेग बिजुलिरु अति खरा॥

sūnya mandire vihārā, rūparekhā nahīm y(j)arā,
duī pada na misai ekapada dharā dharā.

alekhā paṭanā pura, se tabāre tanka gharā,
nahīm saradā usumā sādhujane hetu karā.

nirāmisa niyanta piūthile lage mīṭā,
adekhā anāme svadā se sudhā dhārā.

dekhi ta chātaka chalī, jnāni marucchanti bhali,
chakṣu matakaru vega bijuliru ati kharā.

7. Sunya mandire

He sports in the temple of the void, he has no shape or form!

You can never see his two feet; nevertheless surrender to

Him!

His abode is in that nameless unknown realm!

It is neither too cold nor too warm there! Listen O wise Ones!

He is the untasted, unseen, unnameable nectar, unequalled in sweetness and taste!

Wise Ones keep pondering at his elusive step

Fleeting as the twinkle of an eye and more piercing than lightning!

मध्ये प्रभु विजये, अनामि रखी कये।
अलेखा महिमा, कि देबि उपमा।
अस्रे काले दण्डु आचि पटका॥

वाम दहन कटि, जन्म मृत्यु खटन्ति।
अक्षय पुरुष, भक्तभावे दृश्य।
खैचन्ति अमरिका कलाप॥

एकाक्षर विर्वेद क्षरी असुचि पद।
ब्रह्म निरूपन, होइचि से स्थान।
भणे भीम हिन्द बाई मूरखा॥

madhye prabhu vijaye, anāmi rakhī kaye.
alekhā mahimā, ki debi upamā.
asre kāle daṇḍu āchi paṭakā.

vāma dahana kaṭi, janma mṛtyu khaṭanti.
akṣaya puruṣa, bhakta bhāve dṛśya.
khaichanti amarikā kalāpa.

ekākṣara virveda kṣarī asuchi pada.
brahma nirūpana, hoichi se sthāna.
bhaṇe bhīma hinda bāī mūrakhā.

The Lord shines at the centre of dance, Nameless!
His greatness cannot be described in words,
there is no simile which can compare his radiance!
He wipes away all sins and birth and death.
Let us bow at His feet!
He is immortal and indestructible, can be seen by
devotees through devotion.
No scripture can define his form.
The single letter (Om) recited in divine melody
is His form!
So says Bhima, the worthless idiot.

राग : परास Rāga : Parās

8. स्थावरु जंगम कितरु पतंग चाहिं देले अनुसारी।
सकल घटारे पूरि समनारे नोहे सनबडा करि॥

भावकु निकट अभावे अभेद भक्तभावे पर वासा।
ए मोरा गुहारि न सूना की करि धरि आचा कें रोसा॥

वचनकु एदि भगतिकु छदि अन्यारे की बधिगलि।
प्रभु श्रीचामुरे सेविव पायारे कि कि अपराधकलि॥

न सुनिला परि हेयुंआचा हरिदेवआचा दण्ड सजा।
पखरु अन्तर करि निरन्तर दयारे हेउच्छा दुजा॥

sthāvaru jangama kitaru patanga chāhim dele anusārī,
sakala ghaṭāre pūri samanāre nohe sana baḍā kari.

bhāvaku nikaṭa abhāve abheda bhaktabhāve para vāsā,
e morā guhāri na sūnā kī kari dhari āchā keum rosā.

vacanaku edi bhagatiku chhadi anyāre kī badhigali,
prabhu śrīchāmure seviva pāyāre ki ki aparādha kali.

na sunilā pari heyunāchā hari deva āchā daṇḍa sajā,
pakharu antara kari nirantara dayāre heucchā dujā.

8. Sthavaru jangama

From the immovable to the movable, from insects to birds wherever I look, I find you inhabiting all beings,
Nothing is big or small for you.
It is said that you are near those who beckon you with love,
that you are invisible to those who have no love
and that you are subservient to the devotee's love.
O Lord! why do you not listen to my prayers?
Why are you angry with me?
Have I given up my devotion to you and got involved in other things?
By not listening to my prayers, you seem to punish me!
By driving me away from you you are rendering your compassion negative!

राग : मल्हार | Rāga : Malhār

9. तहङ्कु जेबना जना, निर्वेद करे दर्शना।
अखण्डित ब्रह्मे लिना जन्म मरणरु परा॥

क्रिया कर्मे नलगाई, साधु संग कले पिआ।
दीक्षा त निस्काम धर्म भजन एक अक्षरा॥

यूंथरे ब्रह्मा आच्छि, उदे अस्त नहीं किच्छि।
कहे भीम अरक्षित निगम से अन्धकारा॥

tahanku y(j)ebanā janā, nirveda kare darśanā,
akhaṇḍita brahme linā janma maraṇaru parā.

kriyā karme nalagāī, sādhu sanga kale piā,
dīkṣā ta niskāma dharma bhajana eka akṣarā.

y(j)ūmthare brahmā āchhi, ude asta nahīm kichhi,
kahe bhīma arakṣita nigama se andhakārā.

9. Tahanku jebana

Whoever can visualise Him in silence
merges in the boundless Supreme, crossing the ocean of birth and death.

Actions or deeds are of no avail, only the company of saintly persons helps!
Meditation, duty with detachment and worshipping with focus on the One Letter (OM) help.

Where God reigns,
there is no rising or setting
Says the helpless Bhima:
The darkness is impenetrable!

राग : बिलावल Rāga : Bilāwal

10. अरुण तरसा पडिले येसन अन्धकार यई फटि।
सेहिपरि प्रभु झन खडगारे पटक पाक आ कलि॥

निसिरे चन्द्रमा उदय होईले रजनि करे अलुअ।
सेहि पराकर पाप भर मोरा निवारण करि नीअ॥

सर्पघट हेले गुणिका येसन विसारे पकन्ति पद।
अंगारे मोरा पापलता चातिचि गुरुवुङ्क्ये पौ हद॥

सन्निपात घोटिथिले वैद्यमने मेलन्ति विसन बदि।
मलु अंगारे समुद्र प्राये जल सूखाई त तेज पदि॥

aruṇa tarasā paḍile yesana andhakāra yaee phaṭi,
sehipari prabhu jhana khaḍagāre paṭaka pāka ā kali.

nisire chandramā udaya hoīle rajani kare alua,
sehi parākara pāpabhara morā nivāraṇa kari nīa.

sarpaghaṭa hele guṇikā yesana visāre pakanti pada,
angāre morā pāpalatā chātichi guruvunkye pau hada.

sannipāta ghoṭithile vaidyamane melanti visana badi,
malu angāre samudra prāye jala sūkhāī ta teja padi.

10. Aruṇa tarasa padile

Just as darkness cracks up when sun's rays fall on it
Cut away my sins with the sword of knowledge, O Lord!
When the moon rises at night, light shines everywhere!
Similarly, abolish the burden of my sins, O Lord!
Just as the charmed words of the snake charmer heal the snake bite,
Remove the creepers of sin which have entwined me!
As the doctors remove the causes of approaching death in patients with their poisonous medicines
and masses of water in the patient's body vanish in no time,
so let the ocean of sin vanish from me, O Lord
and let the medicine of knowledge cure me for ever!

SONGS OF NARAYANA GURU

Song	*Raga*
1. Namo nādabindvatmike	Hamsadhwani
2. Jaya jaya candrakaladhara	Sindhubhairavi
3. Niyallo māyayum	Begada
4. Tingalum tridasagangayum	Kharaharapriya
5. Pamparattodu pakaccidum	Sankarabharanam
6. Mupparokkeyita mudijnu	Kamboji
7. Tingalum konnayum	Punnagavarali
8. Ettucuttrodu moksamarga	Todi
9. Eccilcorunda pullikkiniyoru makanam	Shanmukhapriya
10. Pattil pattippuduppuvidalodu	Madhyamavati

NARAYANA GURU

NARAYANA GURU (1856 A.D.-1928 A.D.)

Narayaṇa Guru, the poet-sage and mystic of Kerala, belongs to the land of spiritual teachers like Tirumular, Tiruvalluvar, Sri Ramakrishna Paramahamsa and Ramana Maharishi.

He was born on August 20, 1856 A.D. at Chenpazhanti, north of Tiruvananthapuram (the present capital of Kerala State) in an *Ezhava* family.

He studied Sanskrit under the famous Sanskrit scholar Kammanpally Raman Pillai.

Even from an early age, Nanoo (as he was affectionately called) was introspective and contemplative and preferred solitude and deep thought.

He left home and wandered from place to place in search of spiritual guides and holy places. He spent some time in a cave in a mountain called *Marutwamalai* in Tamil Nadu, where he is believed to have attained enlightenment.

Coming down from the seclusion of the mountain cave, Narayana Guru mixed with people of all castes and religions and proclaimed his famous dictum: "One caste, one religion, one God for man".

Like the Advaitic philosopher, Sankaracharya, Narayana Guru believed in the omnipresence and immanence of God.

In one of his songs, he asks God: "Aren't you illusion, the creator of illusion, the one who sports with illusion and the one who removes illusion?"

Again, like Sạnkaracharya, Narayana Guru has composed beautiful devotional songs to various manifestations of Divinity like Siva, Subramania, Divine Mother, etc.

He attained samadhi on September 20, 1928 at Sivagiri.

राग : हंसध्वनि Rāga : Hamsadhwani

1. नमो नादबिन्द्वात्मिके नाशहीने
नमो नारदादीड्यापादारविन्दे
नमो नान्मायक्कुं मणिप्पूविळक्के
नमो नान्मुखादिप्रियांम्बा नमस्ते ॥

namo naadabindvaatmike naaśaheene
namo nāradaadīḍyāpaadaaravinde
namo naanmaaykkum manippooviḷakke
namo naanmukhaadipriyaambā namaste.

1. Namo nadabindvatmike

   Protrations to you who are in the form of *Nāda* and *Bindu*!
   You are devoid of destruction!
   Your lotus feet are bowed to by Narada and others,
   You are the bejewelled lamp which dispels darkness (of ignorance)!
   Prostrations! O Mother dear to the four-faced Brahma and others!

राग : सिंधु भैरवि Rāga : Sindhu Bhairavi

2. जय जय चन्द्रकलाधर! दैवमे!
जय जय जन्मविनाशन शंकर!
जय जय शैलनिवास सतांपते!
जय जय पालय मामखिलेश्वर॥

जय जय जितकाम जनार्द्दन सेवित!
जय जय शंकर शर्व सनातन!
जय जय मार कळेबर कोमळ!
जय जय साम्ब सदाशिव पाहि मां॥

jaya jaya candrakalaadhara! daivame!
jaya jaya janmavinaaśana śaṃkara!
jaya jaya śailanivaasa sataampate!
jaya jaya paalaya maamakhileśvara.

jaya jaya jitakaama janaardanasevita!
jaya jaya śaṃkara śarva sanaatana!
jaya jaya maarakaḷebara komala!
jaya jaya saamba sadaaśiva paahi maam.

2. Jaya jaya candrakaladhara

O God! who wear the moon on your head! Victory to You! Victory to You!
O Creator of good, who destroy the cycle of births!
Victory to You! Victory to You!
O Lord of the good ones, who reside in the mountains!
Victory to You! Victory to You!
O Lord of everything! Protect me!
Be victorious! Be victorious!
O Conqueror of Cupid!
Who are served by *Janārdana* (Vishnu)
Be Victorious!
O Creator of bliss! O Destroyer! O Eternal One!
Be victorious! Be victorious!
O gentle, handsome Lord! who destroyed Cupid! Be victorious!
Ever-auspicious Lord, accompanied by the Mother!
Protect me!
Victory to You! Victory to You!

राग : बेगडा Rāga : Begaḍā

3. नीयल्लो माययुं माया-
वियायुं मायाविनोदनुं
नीयल्लयो माययै नीक्कि
सायूज्यं नल्कुमार्यनुं
नी सत्यं ज्ञान मानन्दं
नी तन्ने वर्त्तमानवुं
भूतवुं भावियुं वेर-
ल्लोरुं मोऴियु मोर्क्कुकिल् नी!

neeyallo maayayum maayaa-
viyaayum maayaavinodanum
neeyallayo maayayai neekki
saayūjyam nalkumaaryanum
nee satyam jnaanamaanandam
nee tanne varttamaanavum
bhūtavum bhaaviyum vera-
llorum mozhiyu morkkukil nee!

3. Niyallo māyayum

Aren't you illusion, the Creator of illusion and the one who sports with illusion?
Aren't you the One who removes illusion?
Aren't you the noble One who grants liberation?
You are Truth, Knowledge and Bliss!
You are the present, past and future!
You are in all beings!
You are the embodiment of speech!
You are there, whenever I remember you!

राग : खरहरप्रिया Rāga : Kharaharapriyā

4. तिङ्कळुं त्रिदशगंगयुं तिरुमुटि-
क्कणिञ्ञु तेळियिक्कुन्न नल्
तिङ्कळ् नेर्मुखि, दिगम्बरन्ट्रे तिरु-
मेय् पकुत्त शिवमेनिये,
निन् कऴल्क्कमलमेन् करुत्तिल्निल
निर्त्ति नित्य वुमहन्तव-
न्नङ्कुरिच्चरि वऴिञ्ञुपोय् विफल
माय् वरातरुळुकम्बिके!

tinkaḷum tridaśagangayum tirumuṭi-
kkaṇijnu teḷiyikkunna nal
tinkaḷ nermukhi digambaranṭre tiru-
mey pakutta śivameniye,
nin kazhalkkamalamen karuttil nila
nirtti nitya vumahantava-
nnankuriccari vazhijnupoy viphala
maay varaataruḷukambike!

4. Tingalum tridasa gangayum

O Mother!
Who have shared the auspicious body of Siva,
who wears the moon and the celestial Ganga on his head, and who is clothed in space,
Please plant your lotus feet in my consciousness and bless that
my cup of life does not overflow and become wasted.

राग : शंकरभरणं Rāga : Śankarabharaṇam

5. पम्परत्तोडु पकच्चिडुं भ्रमण-
वेगमुळ्ळ मतियोडुव-
न्नम्बरत्तिलज्ञयुन्नतिन्निवन-
शक्तनेन्नु करुतीडु नी
अन्पिरन्नटिकळ् वाऴ्त्तिनिलक्कुमग-
तिक्कु सद्गति वरुत्तीडुं
निन्पाद त्तोडुलयिप्पतिन्नु नियतं
वरं तरुक मंगले!

pamparattoḍu pakacciḍum bhramaṇa-
vegamuḷḷa matiyoḍuva-
nnambarattilajnayunnatinnivana-
śaktanennu karuteeḍu nee
anpirannaṭikaḷ vaazhttinilakkumaga-
tikku sadgati varutteeḍum
nin paadattoḍu layippatinnu niyatam
varam taruka mangale!

5. Pamparattodu pakaccidum

O Auspicious Mother!
Ever grant me the boon that
I,
with mind whirling with a speed higher than the top,
unable
and incompetent to seek refuge in you,
this orphan, worshipping your feet of love
should permanently merge in your feet.

राग : काम्बोजि Rāga : Kāmboji

6. मुप्पारोक्केयिता मुटिज्ञु मुटियिल्
चोल्पोङ्गमप्पुं धरि-
चेप्पोऴुं परमात्म निष्ठयिलिरु-
नीडुन्नु नी येन्तहो!
इप्पारारिनियाळु मिप्परिषयि-
न्नारोडुरय्क्कुन्नु निन्-
तृप्पादत्तणलेन्तिये तुण नमु-
क्कारर्धनारीश्वरा!

muppaarokkeyitaa muṭijnu muṭiyil
colpongumappum dhari-
ceppozhum paramaatma nishṭhayiliru-
neeḍunnu nee yentaho!
ippaaraariniyaaḷu mipparishayi-
nnaaroḍuraykkunnu nin-
tṛppaadattaṇalentiye tuṇa namu-
kkaarardhanāreeśvaraa!

6. Mupparokkeyita

O Ardhanarīsvara! Lord who is half man and half woman!

Please help me reach your holy feet!

Why are you always in deep meditation?

When all the celestials perish

To whom else can people here appeal?

राग : पुन्नागवराळि — Rāga : Punnāgavarāḷi

7. तिङ्कळुं कोन्नयुं चूडुमीशन् पद-
पङ्कजं चेर्न्नुनिन्नाडु पाम्पे
वेण्णीरणिञ्ञु विळङ्ङु तिरुमेनि
कण्णीरोऴुकक्कणाडु पाम्पे!
ओमेन्नु तोट्टोरु कोटिमुन्तप्पोरुळ्
नामेन्नरिञ्ञु कण्डाडु पाम्पे
नादत्तिलुण्डां नमःशिवायप्पोरु-
ळादियायुळ्ळ तेन्नाडु पाम्पे!

tinkaḷum konnayum cooḍumeeśan pada-
pankajam cernnu ninnaaḍu paampe
veṇṇeeraṇijnu viḷangu tirumeni
kaṇṇeerozhukakkaṇaaḍu paampe!
omennu toṭṭoru koṭimuntapporuḷ
naamennarijnu kaṇḍaaḍu paampe
naadattiluṇḍaam namaḥ śivaayapporu-
ḷaadiyaayulla tennaaḍu paampe!

7. Tingalum konnayum

O snake! Dance with the lotus feet of the Lord! who wears the moon and the *Konna** flower!
O snake! Dance seeing the tears flowing on seeing the Divine form which shines wearing ashes!
O snake! Dance knowing that we are the primordial being with its myriad manifestations beginning with the
Pranava sound AUM!
O snake! Dance knowing that the Being who is bowed to as *Namah Sivaya* and present in all sound is the Primal Being!

*A yellow flower, favourite of Siva.

कामने चुट्ट कण्णुल्ल कालारितन्
नामं नुकर्न्नु निन्नाडु पाम्पे
वेळ्ळिमलयिल् विळङ्गुं वेदप्पोरु-
ळुळ्ळिल् कळिक्कुमेन्नाडु पाम्पे!

देहं निजमल्ल देही ओरुवनी
देह त्तिलुण्डरिज्ञीडु पाम्पे
देहवुं देहियुमोन्नायि विळुङ्गीडु-
मेकनुण्डरिज्ञिडु पाम्पे!

kaamane cuṭṭa kaṇṇulla kaalaaritan
naamam nukarnnu ninnaaḍu paampe
veḷḷimalayil viḷangum vedapporu-
ḷuḷḷil kaḷikkumennaaḍu paampe!

deham nijamalla dehee oruvanee
dehattiluṇḍarijneeḍu paampe
dehavum dehiyumonnaayi vizhungeeḍu-
mekanuṇḍarijneeḍu paampe!

O snake! Dance reciting the name of the Enemy of death whose eye burnt Cupid!

O snake! Dance with the knowledge that the Vedic Being who shines in the silvery mountain of Kailasa plays inside us!

O snake! Know that the body is not real and the Spirit is within the body!

O snake! Know that there is One who absorbs both the body and the soul!

राग : तोड़ि Rāga : Toḍi

8. एट्टुचुट्ट्रोडु मोक्षमार्गमिडच्चुमेविन कुण्डली
केट्टरुत्तु किळर्न्नु मण्डलवुं पिळर्न्नु भवत्पदं
तुष्टियोड् पिडिप्पतिन्नरुळन्नतेन्नु भवाब्धियिल्
प्पेट्टु पोकरुतिन्नियुं भगवाने षण्मुख पाहि मां ॥

eṭṭu cuṭṭroḍu mokshamaargamaḍaccumevina kuṇḍalī
keṭṭaruttu kiḷarnnu maṇḍalavum piḷarnnu bhavatpadam
tushṭiyoḍ piḍippatinnaruḷannatennu bhavaabdhiyil
ppeṭṭu pokarutinniyum bhagavaane shaṇmukha paahi maam!

8. Ettu cuttrodu

O six-faced Subrahmanya! Protect me so that
I do not get lost in this ocean of *Samsāra* but
hold on blissfully to your feet,
the Kundalini within me transcending the various blocks
showing me the path to liberation through the eight-fold Yogic way!

राग : षण्मुखप्रिय Rāga : Shaṇmukhapriya

9. एच्चिल् चोरुण्डपुल्लि क्किनियोरु मकनां
नीयिरप्पाळि ज्ञानो
पिच्चक्कारन् पिऴ़य्क्कुं पिऴ़कळखिलवुं
नी पोरुक्केन्नु ज्ञायं
अच्चन् पैतङ्गळ् तन् कालटियिणयटि पे-
ट्रालुमोक्केप्पोरुत्त-
क्कोच्चुङ्गळ् कुल्लभीष्टं कनिवोडु
निर्वेट्रिक्कोडुक्कुन्नुवल्लो ॥

echchil choruṇḍapulli kkiniyoru makanaam
neeyirappaaḷi jnaano
pichchakkaaran pizhaykkum pizhakaḷakhilavum
nee porukkennu jnaayam
achchan paitangaḷ tan kaalaṭiyiṇayaṭi pe-
ṭṭraalumokkepporutta-
kkochchungaḷ kkullabheeshṭaṃ kanivoḍu
niraveṭṭrikkoḍukkunnuvallo!

9. Eccil corunda

You are the son* of the person who eats partly tasted food!

You are the Lord!

I am the beggar!

It is but just that you forgive all the mistakes I commit in earning my livelihood!

Even if the children beat about the feet, the Father fulfils with compassion all the desires of the children!

*Prayer to Lord Subrahmanya.

राग : मध्यमावति Rāga : Madhyamāvati

10. पत्तिल् पत्तिप्पुतुप्पूवितङ्गळोडु पटतल्लुं विरल् तारकङ्गळ्
पत्तुं चित्तं तुळुम्पि च्चोरिच्चमरियनिन्नन् पोळुक्कूरियोडि
सत्तुं चित्तुं कलर्त्तिश्शरवण भव नी
ज्ञानुमायिट्टोरुन्नाळ्
मुत्तुं मुत्तुङ्किरिप्पान् कनक मयिल्-
करेरिक्कळिच्चोटि वा नी ॥

pattilpattipputuppoovitangaḷoḍu paṭatallum viral taarakangaḷ
pattum chittam tuḷumpi chchorichchamariyaninnan pozhukkūriyoḍi
sattum cittum kalarttiśśaravaṇa bhava nee
jnaanumaayiṭṭorunnaaḷ
muttum muttunkirippaan kanaka mayil-
karerikkaḷichchoṭi vaa nee!

10. Pattil patti

O *Saravana bhava*! O Lord Subrahmanya who rose out of

the Saravana pond!

Come sporting on the golden peacock, to play with me,

mixing existence and consciousness,

so that my consciousness blossoms

by contact with your ten starlike fingers

which outrival a hundred new flower petals!